"Customers must recognize that you stand for something."
— Howard Schultz, Starbucks

60-Minute Brand Strategist The Essential Brand Book for Marketing Professionals

For general information about our other products and services, please contact our Customer Care Department within the United States at (800) 762-2974, outside the United States at (317) 572-3993 or fax (317) 572-4002.

Wiley publishes in a variety of print and electronic formats and by print-on-demand. Some material included with standard print versions of this book may not be included in e-books or in print-on-demand. If this book refers to media such as a CD or DVD that is not included in the version you purchased, you may download this material at http://booksupport.wiley.com. For more information about Wiley products, visit www.wiley.com.

Library of Congress Cataloging-in-Publication Data:

Mootee, Idris, 1958-
  60-minute brand strategist: the essential brand book for marketing professionals / Idris Mootee.

    pages cm
    Includes index.

  ISBN 978-1-118-62516-3 (cloth); ISBN 978-1-118-65982-3 (ebk); ISBN 978-1-118-65996-0 (ebk); ISBN 978-1-118-65986-1 (ebk)

  1. Branding (Marketing) I. Title. II. Title: Sixty-minute brand strategist.

HF5415.1255.M676 2013

658.8'27—dc23

                    2013005318

Printed in the United States of America

10 9 8 7 6 5 4 3 2

60-Minute Brand Strategist
The Essential Brand Book for Marketing Professionals

Idris Mootee

Contents

Introduction

This book is a creative compilation of thoughts, processes, frameworks, and visuals taken from my Advanced Branding Master Class, running for more than 10 years in more than 20 countries. This book is for those who haven't yet had the opportunity to attend my seminars. Everyone is busy, with little time to read, so this book is a 60-minute read that could be finished on a flight from New York City to Chicago, or from London to Paris.

Brand is unarguably the most powerful business tool ever invented, after costing and pricing. There are a lot of myths about brand and brand strategy, including the right way to grow the financial and strategic value of a brand and the notion that brand strategy should always align with business strategy. People often place too much value in the power of a logo or a name, but rarely enough on their brand strategy. Many also assume that the brand strategy of larger companies is always robust, and only affordable because of their size. This is far from the truth; every successful business, large or small, global or local, must have a brand strategy and it needn't be complicated.

Many assume a brand's opportunity is only within its product/service category and often forget that the biggest opportunity for growth may exist outside or adjacent to the current definition of the market. All brands should be fighting two wars at the same time—growing existing market share within a defined product category and inventing a new one. The reality is most established product categories brand market shares change very little despite big increases in media spending. So the question is, how can a brand generate growth and create economic value?

For a brand to grow, it requires stepping back from the current situation to develop a systemic way of looking at it from a different viewpoint, then aligning that with business strategy and the competitive context—a robust brand strategy. How can that be used to change the game to your brand's advantage? By bringing empathy into the process, understanding the brand's core and its role in the context of business strategy, and discovering how to change the way customers/channel partners think about the category, not by fighting for incremental share gain within the category.

This little book can help any company succeed by using the brand to inspire and inform a game-changing strategy. Your investment into this book is well worth 60 minutes.

34

15

48

01

x

01
All About Brands

"IN TECHNOCRATIC AND COLORLESS TIMES, BRANDS BRING WARMTH, FAMILIARITY AND TRUST."

—PETER BRABECK, NESTLÉ

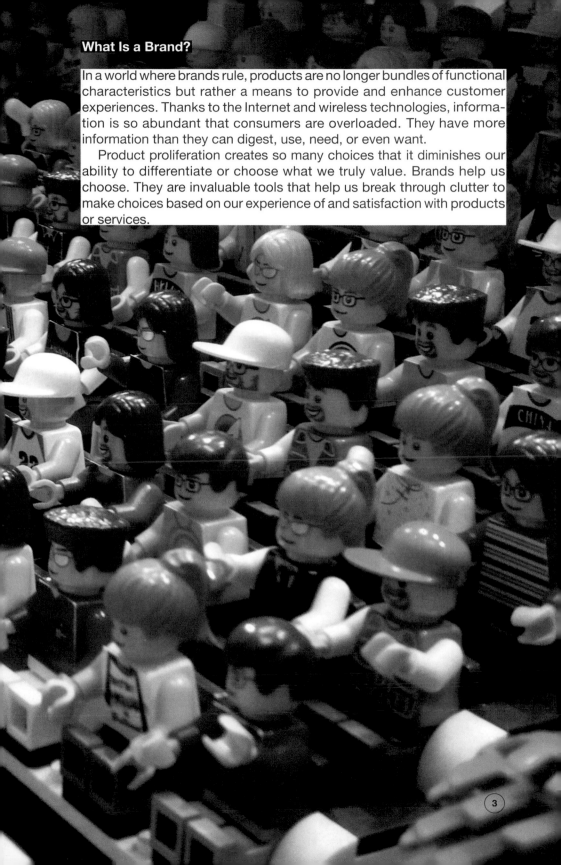

What Is a Brand?

In a world where brands rule, products are no longer bundles of functional characteristics but rather a means to provide and enhance customer experiences. Thanks to the Internet and wireless technologies, information is so abundant that consumers are overloaded. They have more information than they can digest, use, need, or even want.

Product proliferation creates so many choices that it diminishes our ability to differentiate or choose what we truly value. Brands help us choose. They are invaluable tools that help us break through clutter to make choices based on our experience of and satisfaction with products or services.

"There will be a time using a logo will be the worst thing in the world."
—Bill Bernbach, Founder DDB

We're a long long way from that day. The truth is that people like brands. They not only simplify choices and guarantee quality, but they also add fun and interest, provide aspirations and dreams. Some people love them like children, which might explain why I personally know of a 4-year-old boy named Nike, an 8-year-old boy named Ferrari, and a 12-year-old girl named Hermès.

A Brand Is Not ...

A Trademark
(These are legal properties.)

A Mission Statement
(This is a reminder.)

A Logo or Slogan
(These are your signatures.)

A Product or Service
(These are just the tangibles.)

An Advertisement
(These deliver your messages.)

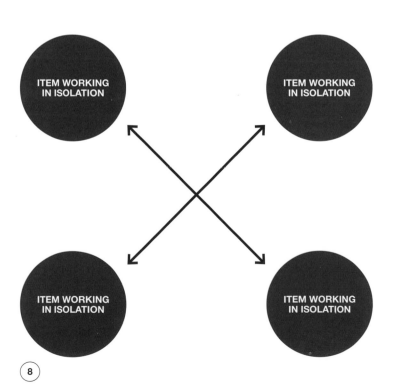

A Brand Is ...

A Point of View
Branding is a strategic point of view,
not a select set of marketing activities.

A Customer Value
Branding is central to creating customer value, not just
sound bites and images.

A Competitive Advantage
Branding is a key tool for creating and sustaining
competitive advantages.

Engineered
Brand strategies must be "engineered" into the strategic
planning process.

Alive
Brands get their identity from meanings. Products
and services are the blood of a brand. Your organizational
culture and standards for action are the heartbeat.

Logic and Emotion
Branding is part science and part art.

A BRAND
IS MORE THAN
THE SUM
OF ITS PARTS.

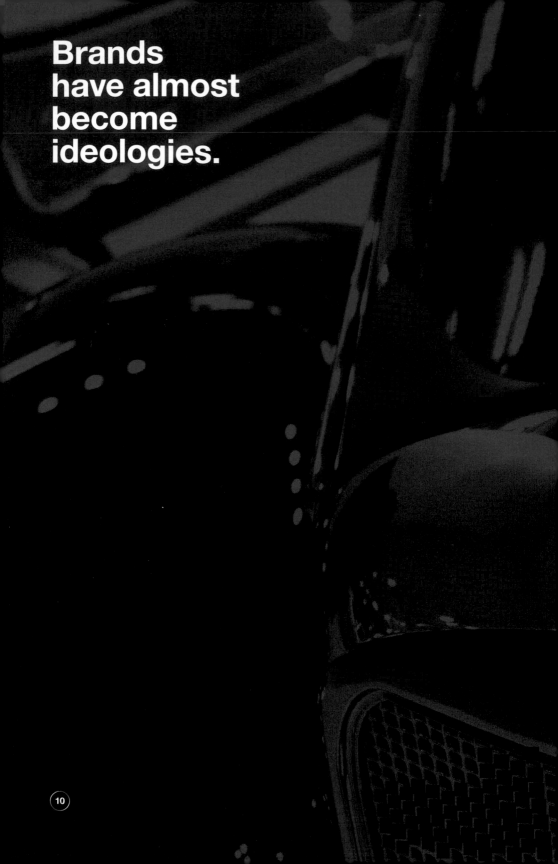

Brands
have almost
become
ideologies.

"The art of marketing is the art of brand building. If you are not a brand, you are a commodity. Then price is everything and the low-cost producer is the only winner."
—Philip Kotler, Kellogg

(13)

"A brand is the 'personification of a product, service, or even entire company.'

Like any person, a brand has a physical 'body': in P&G's case, the products and/or services it provides. Also, like a person, a brand has a name, a personality, character and a reputation.

Like a person, you can respect, like and even love a brand. You can think of it as a deep personal friend, or merely an acquaintance. You can view it as dependable or undependable; principled or opportunistic; caring or capricious. Just as you like to be around certain people and not others, so also do you like to be with certain brands and not others.

Also, like a person, a brand must mature and change its product over time. But its character, and core beliefs shouldn't change. Neither should its fundamental personality and outlook on life.

People have character ... so do brands. A person's character flows from his/her integrity: the ability to deliver under pressure, the willingness to do what is right rather than what is expedient. You judge a person's character by his/her past performance and the way he/she thinks and acts in both good times, and especially bad.

The same are true of brands."
—Robert Blanchard,
former P&G executive

To plan for one year,
grow sales.

To plan for three years,
grow channels.

To plan for decades,
grow a brand.

VALUE

SALES

CHANNEL

BRAND

0 1 2 3 4 5 6 7 8 9 10 11 12 13 14 15 16 17 18 19 20 21 22 23 24 25 26 ...

YEARS

In today's hyper-competitive and über-connected world, it is necessary for brands to have a clear purpose and meaning for consumers. An authentic brand comes from within. It is the exposure of what a company really is. A few interactions with the company will quickly reveal if their marketing and branding is simply saying what they think will appeal rather than what they think and believe. Brands run into problems with social media when there is a lapse between what consumers expect, how the company behaves, and what they promise.

"Be yourself; everyone else is already taken."
—Oscar Wilde, Author & Playwright

"True cultural connection is the Holy Grail for brands if they want to create an enduring emotional relationship with people."
—Adam Chmielowski

"Your vision will become clear only when you look into your heart… Who looks outside, dreams. Who looks inside, awakens."
—Carl Jung

01
What is the deep need that we satisfy? What is our raison d'être?

02
What is our core competence? What are we really good at?

The Customer Satisfaction Treadmill

Daniel Kahneman of Princeton describes the Customer Satisfaction Treadmill. The more we make, the more we spend, the more we want. The faster we get it, the faster we want it. The more convenient it becomes, the more we realize how convenient it could be. The more our unreasonable demands are met, the more unreasonable they become.

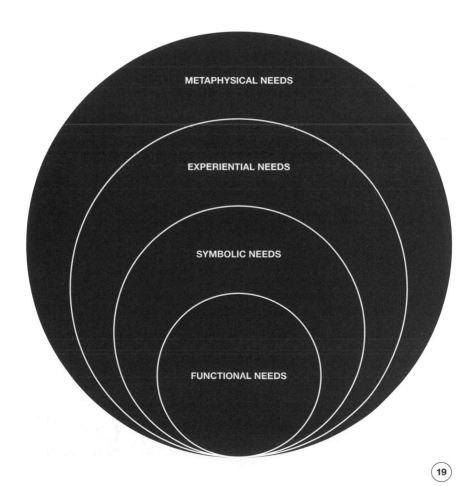

METAPHYSICAL NEEDS

EXPERIENTIAL NEEDS

SYMBOLIC NEEDS

FUNCTIONAL NEEDS

Brand Taxonomies

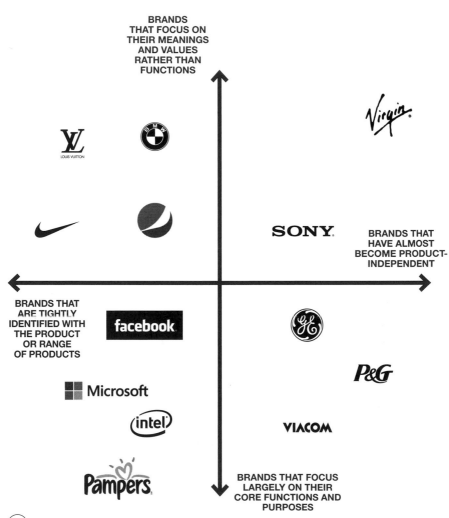

BRANDS
THAT FOCUS ON
THEIR MEANINGS
AND VALUES
RATHER THAN
FUNCTIONS

BRANDS THAT
HAVE ALMOST
BECOME PRODUCT-
INDEPENDENT

BRANDS THAT
ARE TIGHTLY
IDENTIFIED WITH
THE PRODUCT
OR RANGE
OF PRODUCTS

BRANDS THAT FOCUS
LARGELY ON THEIR
CORE FUNCTIONS AND
PURPOSES

Brand Meaning

In a world predisposed to sameness, there are few things in life more satisfying than building brands that disrupt predisposition. Brands move market share. Brands move advertising-award judges. Brands move culture. Some do all of these.

Brand has meaning in people's minds that exists beyond functionality. Part art, part science, brand is the difference between a bottle of soda and a bottle of Coke, a computer and an iMac, a cup of coffee and a cup of Starbucks, a car and a Mercedes, a designer's handbag and a Hermès Birkin. Brand is the intangible yet visceral impact of a person's subjective experience with the product, the personal memories and cultural associations that orbit around it. Brands are also about messages—strong, exciting, distinct, authentic messages that tell people who you are, what you think, and why you do what you do.

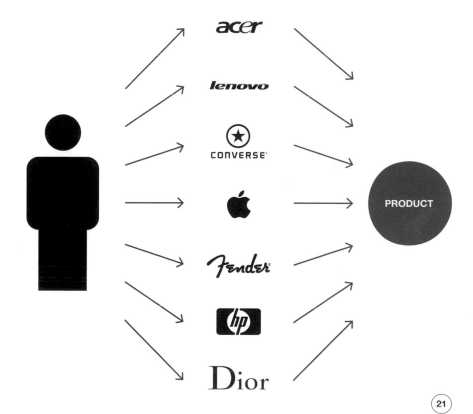

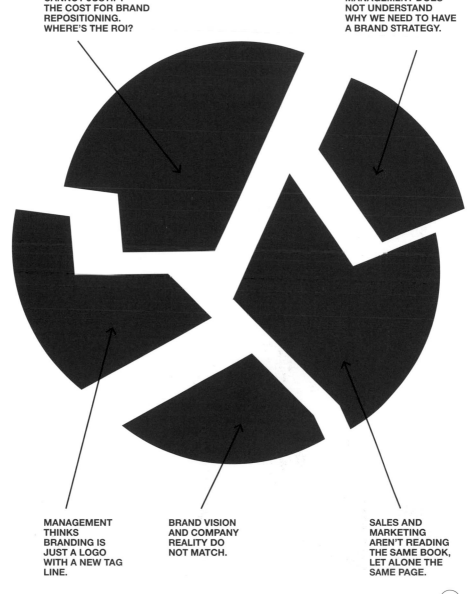

CANNOT JUSTIFY
THE COST FOR BRAND
REPOSITIONING.
WHERE'S THE ROI?

MANAGEMENT DOES
NOT UNDERSTAND
WHY WE NEED TO HAVE
A BRAND STRATEGY.

MANAGEMENT
THINKS
BRANDING IS
JUST A LOGO
WITH A NEW TAG
LINE.

BRAND VISION
AND COMPANY
REALITY DO
NOT MATCH.

SALES AND
MARKETING
AREN'T READING
THE SAME BOOK,
LET ALONE THE
SAME PAGE.

Why Brands Are in Trouble?

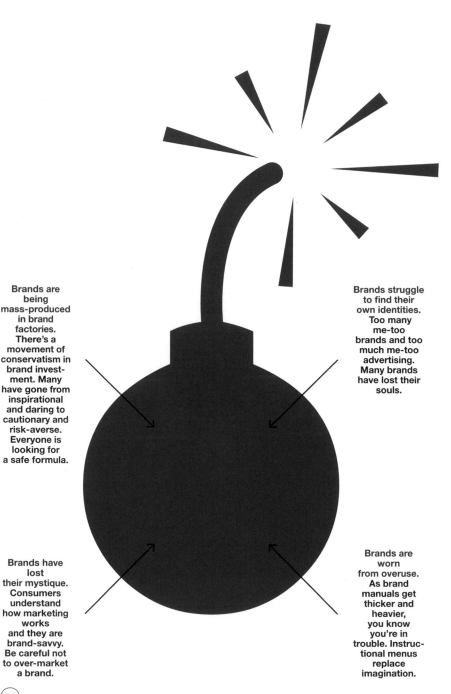

Brands are being mass-produced in brand factories. There's a movement of conservatism in brand investment. Many have gone from inspirational and daring to cautionary and risk-averse. Everyone is looking for a safe formula.

Brands struggle to find their own identities. Too many me-too brands and too much me-too advertising. Many brands have lost their souls.

Brands have lost their mystique. Consumers understand how marketing works and they are brand-savvy. Be careful not to over-market a brand.

Brands are worn from overuse. As brand manuals get thicker and heavier, you know you're in trouble. Instructional menus replace imagination.

What Is a Brand?

Don't make the mistake of letting brand image take over and become brand identity. It's only part of the equation, not the answer.

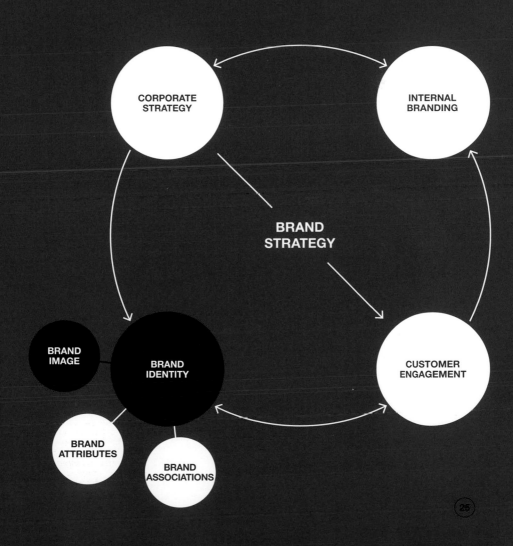

What Is a Brand?

A brand is an intangible asset that resides in people's hearts and minds. It's defined by the expectations people have about tangible and intangible benefits that they develop over time through communications and, more important, actions! To build a successful brand you must do the following four things:

01 Make a promise
02 Communicate your promise
03 Keep your promise
04 Strengthen your promise

The tangible aspect of your brand is a promise. What do you do best? What's the payoff? What can your consumer count on? This promise becomes an intrinsic part of your marketing message. In order for you to own it, you must communicate strategically and creatively across a broad media mix. Both your internal and external audiences must be true believers of your promise. The only way to make them truly believe is to be true about your promise.

Today you may have a name and a trademark, but it will take time (and much more) before you have a brand. Brand building is the creation and management of inward cash flow, with brand equity as the savings account. Managing brand is about how marketers and consumers collaborate to create meaning. Brand building is not an option. ROI is only relevant when considering alternative marketing programs. Brand equity is a big elephant: looking at financial returns alone is unacceptable. You must understand the whole beast.

What Is a Brand?

The trust-based, value-producing relationship called a *brand* is proof that the company is organizationally aligned to repeat the process and sustain the values.

01 Find and establish your niche. Clarify your distinct ability to make an impact.

02 Determine the desired relationship between your customers/prospects and your product.

03 Create intangible, emotional bonds through every customer interaction.

04 Like people, a brand requires a name, a personality, a character, and a reputation.

Brand management is a crucial element of corporate strategy rather than solely a marketing function. It helps a company break away from the pack in creating shareholder value. Brand strategy is the viable expression of business strategy.

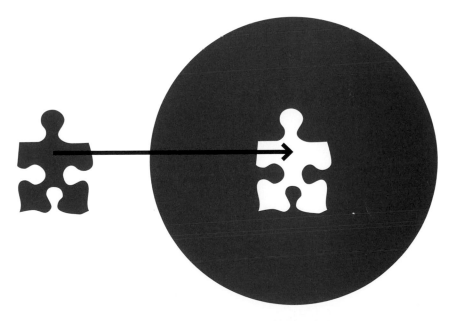

BRAND STRATEGY   CORPORATE STRATEGY

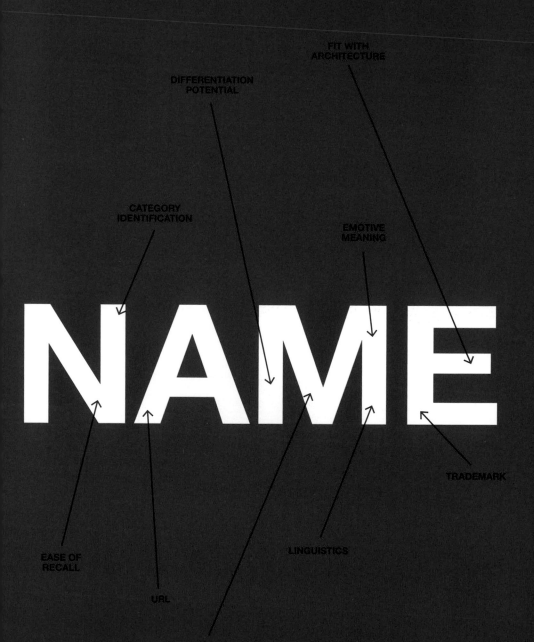

FIT WITH
ARCHITECTURE

DIFFERENTIATION
POTENTIAL

CATEGORY
IDENTIFICATION

EMOTIVE
MEANING

NAME

TRADEMARK

EASE OF
RECALL

LINGUISTICS

URL

ELEMENT OF BRAND
ARCHITECTURE

What Is a Brand Worth?

That depends on whom
you ask. Two research firms,
using less than scientific
methods, can often come up
with different values. Here
are the most recent brand
values for selected companies.

- Millward Brown
- Interbrand

🍎
$33.5 B
$183 B

𝒟ISNEY
$17.1 B
$29 B

IKEA
$9.2 B
$11.9 B

AMERICAN
EXPRESS
$14.6 B
$20.2 B

✔ (Nike)
$14.5 B
$16.3 B

TOYOTA
$21.8 B
$27.8 B

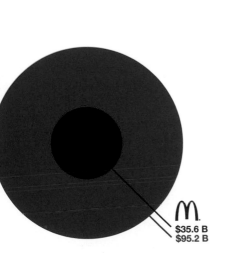

M.
$35.6 B
$95.2 B

Coca-Cola
$71.9 B
$74.3 B

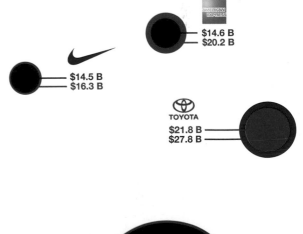

"The brand image always comes first, and fostering that culture within a label should be done through trusting, honest relationships within the company to ensure everyone is working toward a single vision. Transforming the 156-year-old British luxury goods company into a global digital

storyteller of the brand

has required a solid set of strategic initiatives, including centralized supply chain operations to improve product and content distribution agility, reorganization to break down barriers of communication between key executives, and new departments and governance councils to facilitate innovative creative thinking."
—Angela Ahrendts,
CEO, Burberry

Brand Extensions Brand Equity Enhancement (or Dilution) Index

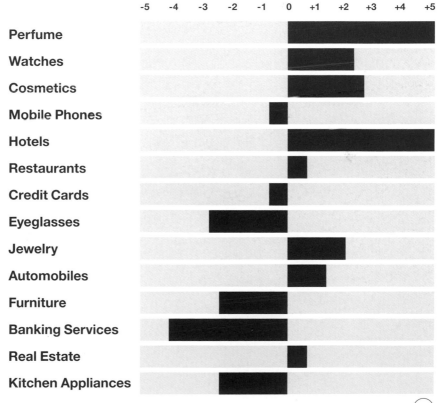

	-5	-4	-3	-2	-1	0	+1	+2	+3	+4	+5
Perfume											
Watches											
Cosmetics											
Mobile Phones											
Hotels											
Restaurants											
Credit Cards											
Eyeglasses											
Jewelry											
Automobiles											
Furniture											
Banking Services											
Real Estate											
Kitchen Appliances											

Mind over Matter

Psychological differences may seem insubstantial, but in terms of sustainability, they are often more resilient than functional differences.

Intangible emotional associations are difficult to copy: Once an emotional territory is occupied by a well-known brand, it is more difficult to displace than a brand with a functional association.

Built to Last

Advantages built on emotional values and brand meanings (e.g., Levi's, Nike, Starbucks, Amazon, BMW, Harley-Davidson, Apple, Sony) are often the most durable.

PERSONALITY   TRUST

TIMELESSNESS   UNIQUENESS

A product is built in a factory ... A brand is built in trust and relationships

A product is easily copied by a competitor ... A brand is unique

A product is an object ...
A brand is a personality

A product is sold by a
merchant ... A brand is
bought by a customer

A product is quickly
outdated ... A brand is
timeless

35

Mind over Matter

Without their brand, Apple would have died. The power of their brand kept them alive during the mid-1990s when their products were lackluster. Their brand bought them time until they came out with the next runaway hit—the iMac.

For Apple, the brand is always bigger than the product. It is an ideology, a value set. Apple is about imagination, innovation, and individualism.

It's not just about advertising or visual identity. Brands must be built 360 degrees. Branding means that collateral information, meaning, association, and value have been spliced into the very DNA of the brand. This has two core components: label and fable. *Label* refers to all visual elements, packaging, and taglines. *Fable* refers to the extrinsic aspect of branding attached from the outside, most often from customer experiences, advertising, corporate trust, and customer relationships. The brand is the totality of what the customer experiences: the look and feel of your office, your community reputation, your awning and signage, your sales and customer service people, and the way you handle business conflicts and customer complaints.

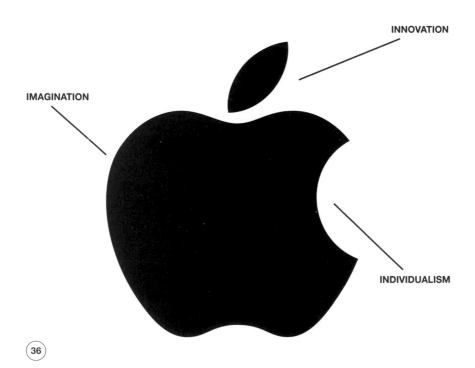

Branding is often confused with an advertising campaign or a corporate identity. Companies are still turning to branding as a panacea. Equally problematic are the self-proclaimed branding experts happy to sell you pricey snake oil. In novice hands, branding becomes a way to obfuscate relative sameness or make promises that can't be fulfilled, rather than communicating relevant uniqueness and building trust and credibility.

Three key requirements for building strong brands:

01 **Trust between brand and consumer**

02 **Common identity between brand and consumer**

03 **Point of difference between brands in a set**

17

25

31

04

38

Branding in a Postmodern Culture

45

56

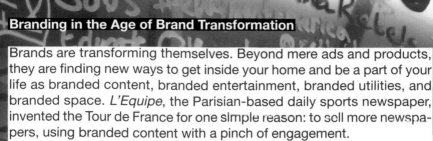

Brands are transforming themselves. Beyond mere ads and products, they are finding new ways to get inside your home and be a part of your life as branded content, branded entertainment, branded utilities, and branded space. *L'Equipe*, the Parisian-based daily sports newspaper, invented the Tour de France for one simple reason: to sell more newspapers, using branded content with a pinch of engagement.

But customers are transforming brands, too. New cultural modes of performance are emerging from new network-based social behaviors and conversations. With more than 50 million people able to share ideas, opinions, and experiences in a single online space—and generate billions of web page impressions every month—these behaviors and conversations are creating a seismic shift in the traditional balance of power that once existed between customers and companies.

As content is increasingly delivered via personalized and self-scheduled social webs, viewers—not broadcasters—will decide when, how, why, and what is consumed. And they will dictate who they share that consumption with.

The question is, what role should brand play in this age of transformation?

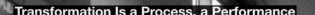

Transformation Is a Process, a Performance

To make the story of a brand complete and meaningful, it requires that all of the actors—customers and companies alike—successfully complete transitions from scene to scene and stage to stage. In today's script, those transitions read like this:

Interruption is the stage where old scripts get shredded, rules get tossed out the window, and the paradigms we lived by are revealed as obsolete. The Internet is our Interruption. It has forever ruptured the old system of brand control and communication.

Intrusion is the stage between what was and what will be. A wild zone of new ideas and new rituals, it is alive with uncertainty, excitement, and expectation. This gestative space where customers and companies create and explore brand futures is where we are right now.

Engagement is the curtain call of this performance. A celebration of the new reality and the ideas and rituals that brought it to life, brands that will occupy center stage are those that contribute the new ideas, help facilitate the new rituals, meet the new needs, and, ultimately, tell the best stories. Those who ignore this new reality do so at their own peril.

Mind over Matter

When distribution is trivial, unlimited, and available to all, marketing to a captive audience sitting on a couch in front of a television or radio is a thing of the past. In fact, this kind of old-world marketing has become adversarial to customers. Having adapted to the media-fragmented and always-on new reality, they seek value by searching, discovering, and sharing their very personal brand caches with peers—not waiting for you to interrupt them with unwanted messaging.

Broadcasting is in trouble, and user-generated videos are just the beginning. The social-casting of YouTube will evolve and, in the process, so too will consumer behavior. Instead of passivity, the experience flow of tomorrow will be characterized by immediacy, flexibility, portability, permeability, fluidity, interactivity, mashability, and ownerability.

With the emergence and convergence of the mobile phone, the Internet, and location-based systems, consumers also have immediate access to co-workers, friends, and family members. Between getting used to and being born into a connected age, they are naturally and increasingly drawing on participation in various networks for information, assistance, support, and recommendations.

Creating great products, services, and content is paramount. Content? Yes, content. An integral part of any product or service and their related experiences, customers will consume only what's relevant to them, what best serves them, and what truly entertains them—not what is marketed to them by you through repetition. Engaging them will require branded experiences rich in content that strengthen contextual involvement and consumer connection. Within such experiences, the density and intensity of polysemic, multi-origin, co-created, and fragmented communication will make Baudrillard's hyper-reality seem as antiquated as TV.

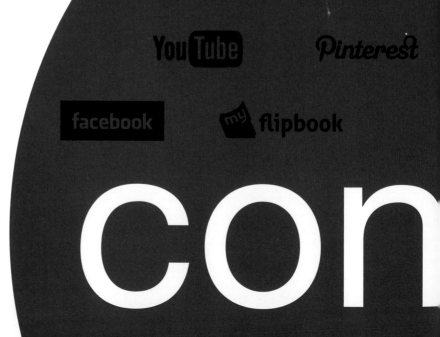

Content Is Everything

Great content—the kind that truly engages—helps customers tell a story, perform a part of their life, communicate meaning to others, and be all that they can be. It is, quite simply, cultural.

In the past, the clearest demonstration of content (and brands) as cultural was in the subculture. Punks, mods, ravers, skaters, church-goers, artists, bikers, and others made commodities come to life through performances like no other consumers on earth. Today, because of the scope and reach of social media, we are in an age of the post-subcultural. The Hipster, a mash-up of subcultural traditions, has become the emblem of insider-ness made accessible to all with the Internet.

Just as subculturalists were the creative class of brand dissemination, modification, alteration, and transformation, so now are the millions of people around the world who, through social media, have access to insider knowledges, practices, experiences, performances, and collaborative communities.

This occurs through YouTube, Flickr, Twitter, Facebook, and the thousands of online advice, support, co-creation, and retail portals. The relentless virtualization of social life, the marketing of niche-interactions, the sharing of experiences, and the outsourcing of work means that less and less of our daily lives are produced and consumed at home. Rather, we are performing ourselves more in public, more collaboratively, and more than ever, through the kinds of social networks that once existed solely in subcultures.

Google+

Instagram

flickr™

twitter

tent

The Personal Brand

In the age of the Personal Brand, commoditization is permeating every aspect of daily life. Style, taste, identity, and individuality have become central to what we expect from our experiences in health care, learning, dating, news, clothing, food, travel, home furnishings, communication, sports, entertainment, sexuality, spirituality, birth, marriage, babies, and burials. Twenty years ago, in the social mainstream, this wasn't the case. Sub-culturalists were picky about their purchases, but the average consumer had a less refined sense of assembling their self through products and services.

Today, instant communication has blown the doors off the old-world media and advertising industry. Taste gurus, microbrands, blogs, chatters, Friends, Tweeters, citizen journalists, and the searchability of style have forever changed the how, what, where, when, and why of consumption. In the new free-for-all of ideas, opinions, reviews, and experiences, individuals with greater access to information strive to define and display their Personal Brand, niche is the norm, cool is hyper-commoditized, and branding becomes as much a bottom-up phenomenon for customers as a top-down priority for companies.

One result is that we have become desperate to socialize the profane. Distracted by the pace of change, unfulfilled in our personal lives, and feeling disempowered by our work, many of us turn to celebrities, rock stars, designers, and brands to cultivate more meaning in life. But when work is empowering and life is meaningful, interest and engagement in high-consumption lifestyles will wane. De-marketing will happen. Until then, a brand's role is to help to create meanings in everyday life through commodities.

Many companies are simply not ready to deal with or anticipate identity obsolescence in the same way they anticipate the obsolescence of products or business models. Despite the best efforts of management teams, many can't adapt to shifts in the competitive environment because the required brand-driven adaptive response is inconsistent with the company's core identity. Any brand exercise will only widen the gap between the brand and the corporate core identity.

"We spent eight months and a lot of money on a brand strategy and all that's changed is the logo and tagline." —CEO, Financial Services Company

"We hired a brand consultant and developed a great brand strategy. Our ad agency went on to create and produce an ad campaign that far exceeded our capability to deliver the brand promise. We ended up with disappointed customers, internal conflicts and brand credibility erosion." —CEO, Telco

Zombie Brands, Dinosaur Brands, Ghost Brands, or Graveyard Brands are what people used to call brands that customers have either completely abandoned or that are simply hanging on by a thread, usually at the Dollar Store or at Costco in a totally unrelated product category. Some have gone through unsuccessful revitalization efforts, others exist only in emerging markets, and a few have simply lost relevance in their core market place (Xerox, Oldsmobile) and are used casually on products totally outside their product category (Teac, RCA, Polaroid, etc.).

If you happen to own a Zombie Brand, what can you do?

01 Invest and attempt to revitalize it
02 Milk it
03 Position it for the emerging market
04 Sell it for whatever it's worth
05 Dump it

Consumers with special relationships with Zombie Brands often have sentimental reasons for continuing to make purchases or giving them a second chance. But the cost and risk of bringing a brand back to life is enormous. If this is your choice, make sure the decision to do so is based on sound logic. If you run a large portfolio, the questions will be: Which brands are worth the revitalization effort? And why?

Many B-school case studies have chronicled brands brought back from the dead. But for every success, there are hundreds of failures: companies that tried to revitalize old brands by hiring new agencies and throwing endless amounts of money into advertising in hopes of rebuilding, even when there wasn't a relevant product, or service, or sound strategy behind the initial move. How bad is your situation? Here are the three most common scenarios:

My brand is sick.

Market changes direction and the brand becomes irrelevant. Everyone (advertising, product design, promotions) used to understand what the brand means and they all stick to it, believing it connects to something larger and more enduring. But one day they wake up and realize there is a big disconnect. Your brand is stuck in the past. **Your brand is irrelevant.**

My brand is dying.

The brand is becoming boring. It doesn't create excitement for customers or even employees anymore. Younger consumers think of it as their parents' brand. This is common with brands that have been successful and achieved market leadership. In fact, it's often the result of being too successful. Your successful past has made you lazy. **Your brand lacks customer engagement.**

My brand has no vital signs.

You've ignored your brand for too long or simply let it ride to expiry. Every drop of energy and goodwill has been squeezed out. It has lost its power to capture your customers' (or even your own) imaginations. Your brand is a shell. **It has been reduced to nothing more than a logo.**

Can social media save the Zombie Brands?

The Social Media Generation has phenomenal influence over the fate of brands. Active, mobile, and vocal, they share the joys, angers, and frustrations of their daily experiences with anybody and everybody. In doing so, their digital connectivity becomes the web that weaves Brand Communities. Separated by their geography but bound by their love of a particular brand, citizens of these communities can be identified by four core markers:

01 Shared Interests
02 Shared Values
03 Shared Rituals
04 Shared Purposes

The commercial, mass-mediated ethos in which Brand Communities are situated affects their character and structure and gives rise to their particularities. From a brand and marketing perspective, this is the most disruptive trend. It means that social media, not advertising, has become the conduit for communication, and that customers are the collective source of truth for brands. Given the right new content, the Brand Community is a possible cure for the Zombie Brand.

Brand Evolution

Sometimes successful rebranding requires "evolution" more than "revolution." It is easier to contemporize a tired brand than to introduce a completely new brand design, unless there is a strong reason to do so. It is important to retain the fragile emotional ties and customer loyalty that has taken years to build.

The Batman brand stands for brave choices, powerful wisdom, and a call to action. When the young Bruce Wayne kneels by his bed and prays, "And I swear by the spirits of my parents to avenge their deaths by spending the rest of my life warring on all criminals," he is articulating Batman's brand promise.

Branding Gets Metaphysical

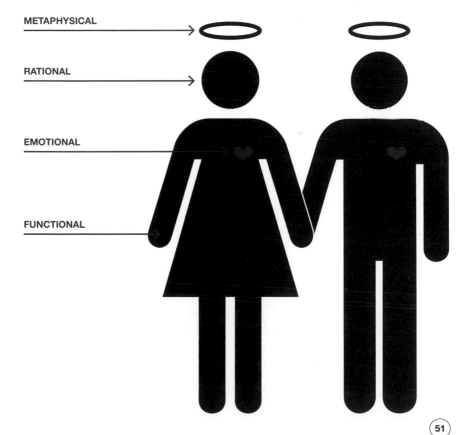

METAPHYSICAL

RATIONAL

EMOTIONAL

FUNCTIONAL

Brand Culture

Your brand is your culture and your culture is your brand. This is how brand equity is built. Brands have always had close relationships with organizational culture. An appropriate and well-aligned culture can provide a brand with a sustainable competitive advantage. It's not so much about how customers value what they receive, but how it's being delivered. Brand-driven organizational culture is about having the motivation and inspiration to be different.

"At Zappos, our belief is that if you get the culture right, most of the other stuff—like great customer service, or building a great long-term brand, or passionate employees and customers—will happen naturally on its own.

We believe that your company's culture and your company's brand are really just two sides of the same coin. The brand may lag the culture at first, but eventually it will catch up.

Your culture is your brand."
— Tony Hsieh, CEO, Zappos

Zappos formally defined their
brand culture in 10 core values:

01 Deliver WOW Through Service
02 Embrace and Drive Change
03 Create Fun and a Little Weirdness
04 Be Adventurous, Creative,
   and Open-Minded
05 Pursue Growth and Learning
06 Build Open and Honest Relationships
   with Communication
07 Build a Positive Team and
   Family Spirit
08 Do More with Less
09 Be Passionate and Determined
10 Be Humble

24

80

16

42

Strategic Perspectives of Branding

"We have a surplus of similar companies, employing similar people, with similar educational backgrounds, working in similar jobs, coming up with similar ideas, producing similar things, with similar prices and similar quality."
—Kjell Nordstrom and Jonas Ridderstrale, Funky Business

"We also have a surplus of similar brands, having similar attributes, with similar marketing messages and slogans, coming up with similar brand claims, with similar quality, selling at similar prices. Welcome to the surplus economy!"
—Idris Mootee

Dolly the Sheep

Brand Attention Deficit

The average consumer is exposed to as many as 500 to 2,000 branded messages per day. Multiple studies indicate that less than 10 percent of prime time ads have clear positioning. Between 2000 and 2010, the number of new packaged goods introduced globally increased by more than 20 percent, the largest increase in a decade. Most of these were "me-too" products destined to be lost in the crowd and to reduce some brands to a near-commodity status.

With the proliferation of smartphones and tablets resulting in explosion in video consumption which is estimated to grow at a rate of 30 to 40 percent over the next 5 years. More screens in more places and more interactions between viewers and brands. Brand marketers understand the need for "emotional connection" and "story," mining so-called trends and the cultural zeitgeist to identify that magical hook that will make consumers remember their brands. The key is to deepen the provenance, development, and heritage that defines who people are, where we belong, how we behave, and why we have come to value the things we do and create the world the way that we have.

In a world where brands abound, competition is increasingly intense and the speed of competitive responses is ever shorter. The race is on to rise above the throng of brands, sustain presence, and maintain relevance and customer loyalty. But all too often, companies fall into the trap of thinking short-term, being overly ambitious for short-term results or lacking a robust brand strategy.

NOT ONLY ARE BRANDS SIMILAR, EVEN THE COMPANIES ARE NOW MORE OR LESS THE SAME

Branding and McDonaldization

McDonaldization is everywhere. Individualism and diversity are replaced by efficiency and social control. It is the process by which the principles of the fast food restaurant dominate more and more sectors of our society throughout the world.

McDonald's has 30,000 restaurants in 121 countries, 60 percent of which are outside the USA. Shopping centers are everywhere and the shops and merchandise are mostly the same. This trend is visible in many other businesses, from toys, auto-repair, convenience stores, and consumer electronics, to books and general merchandise. The "control" and "system" components are key. Replacement of human by non-human technology is often oriented toward greater control and more consistent quality. The great source of uncertainty and unpredictability in a rationalizing system is people — either the people who work within those systems or the people who are served. Branding advertising is used to put the human elements back. The warm and smiling faces in TV commercials are intended to convince customers about "calculability"* over "individuality."

* "(calculability) involves an emphasis on things that can be calculated, counted, quantified. Quantification refers to a tendency to emphasize quantity rather than quality. This leads to a sense that quality is equal to a certain, usually (but not always) large quantity of things."
—George Ritzer, *The McDonaldization of Society*

Economic Evolution

In the surplus economy, the marketing battle is a battle of the brands—a competition for brand dominance. Companies will recognize that brands are a company's most valuable assets and that it is more important to own markets than factories.

Brands are blurring the distinction between art, commerce, culture, and life, and our economy, behaviors, and culture are all threads in the patchwork of human experience. A tweet is an act of expressing, sharing, promoting, and shaping. Social media allow brands to enrich culture, social creativity, and human values while social technology can leverage brand heritage to reframe our cultural context in intriguing and exciting new ways.

The only way to own markets is to own market-dominant brands. The brand battlefield that used to be confined in the world of media advertising is now fought on new ground where the rules are being redefined. Consumers have grown wary of advertising because the majority of it lacks credibility and authenticity. Brands had a poor record of delivering their promises through advertising and had been disappointed with reality. There is the overlapping space between the products, service, and the experiences, where the messaging ends and the experience begins.

The Battle of Brands

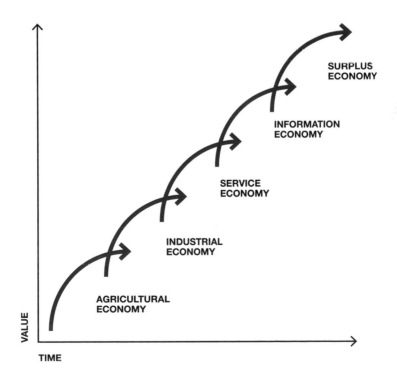

VALUE

SURPLUS ECONOMY

INFORMATION ECONOMY

SERVICE ECONOMY

INDUSTRIAL ECONOMY

AGRICULTURAL ECONOMY

TIME

Most businesses have a relationship with their customers that is based solely on price. That is why so many companies are having difficulties maintaining their margins. The challenge is to figure out how to extend those transaction-based relationships to emotion-based relationships. Professor Susan Fournier at Harvard Business School has classified the relationships consumers have with their brands into fifteen types ranging across the whole spectrum. They include:

Committed Partnership
Usually long-term and voluntary relationship: a man is so involved with his brand of bicycle that he becomes an advocate of it, singing its praises to his friends.

Enslavement
Involuntary relationship governed exclusively by the partner's wishes or desires: a consumer is unhappy with the local cable provider but has no alternative source for the service.

Fournier's Approach:

Meet with consumers (hundreds of people over several years) to listen to their life stories, discover their interests and goals, and hear about the ups and downs of their daily lives. Then ask each person to describe his/her "brand portfolio" and to explain why they choose the products they do.

Fournier drew out seven essential attributes of good brand relationship quality:

Interdependence
Brand is inextricably woven into consumers' daily life and routine.

Love and passion
Consumers feel affection/passion for the products and may experience separation anxiety if it is not available.

Commitment
Consumers stick with the product through good or bad times either in his or her lifestyle or in the product's life cycle.

Self-concept connection
Using the brand helps consumers address a life issue, such as a need to belong or a fear of growing old.

Intimacy
Consumers describe a sense of deep familiarity with the product and an understanding of its attributes.

Partner quality
Consumers seek certain positive traits in the brand such as dependability, trust, worthiness, and accountability—the same qualities as one would look for in a best friend.

Nostalgic attachment
Brand brings back memories either because it was used at an earlier time in life or because it was associated with loved ones.

Customer Relationships

Managing customer relationships has become managing software vendor relationships. So, what went wrong? Shouldn't companies be putting their money back into developing the "R" of "CRM"?

Marketers and "CRM" vendors set unrealistically high expectations when they talk about "relationships." Should they be using a different word instead?

"A good relationship is an asset. We can invest in relationships, and we can borrow from them. We all do it but almost never manage it. Yet a company's most precious asset is its relationship with customers."
—Theodore Levitt, Harvard Business School

"Traditionally, tactical marketing decisions— regarding packaging and advertising, for instance—are made by different people or departments. A holistic understanding of the relationship that consumers have with a brand can give direction to a company's marketing activities and result in a stronger bond between consumer and brand"
—Susan Fournier, Harvard Business School

Rise and Rise of the Brand

The very technologies that make it faster, easier, and cheaper to innovate also help us to imitate. The game switched from innovation to imitation. The increasing difficulty in differentiating between products and services, and the speed with which competitors take up innovations will only assist in the rise and rise of the brand. Many of our dreams and desires for a better world are no longer articulated by John Kennedys or Martin Luther Kings, or generated through personal epiphanies—they are now the intellectual currency of brands. When brands connect to inspiration and epiphany—personal, collective, or conjured by leaders—they enter into a realm immune to imitation.

Decision Map
for Brand Choices

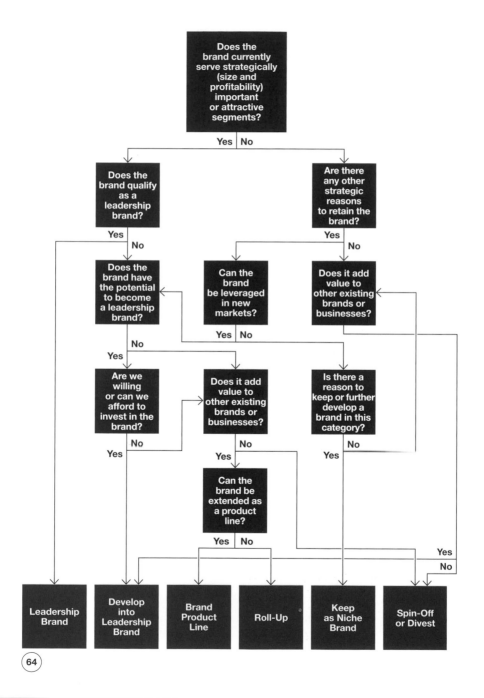

Decision Map
for Brand Leveraging

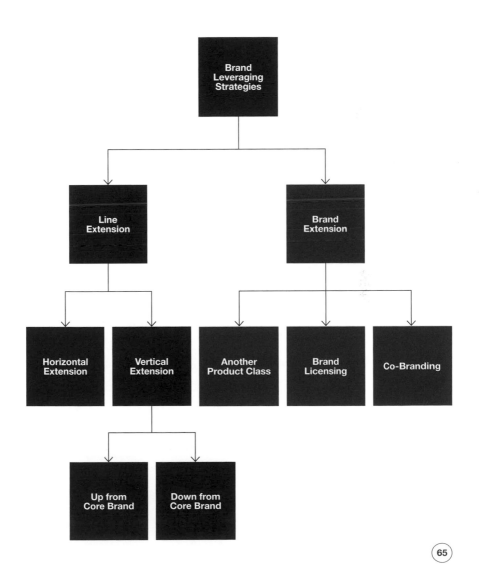

Branding Challenges

The challenge for brand management is finding ways of connecting with customers that provide value, substance, significance, meaning, and usefulness beyond their current product and service definition and those offered competitively. This requires deep understanding of people's lives. It means being smarter at developing real relationships. It also must be a dynamic process in keeping up with changes in ever-changing customer wants and needs. One of the real keys to long-term brand success is investing so customers like us, trust us, value us, keep coming back to us, are willing to pay a premium for us, and choose to take us into their lives.

For the most part, however, today's organizations work against this type of brand success. The designs of most business organizations are disaggregated. Customers don't think or act in organizational silos, but organizations do. This often blocks true understanding. How can we ever hope to understand customers when we only concern ourselves with a small part of their lives, attitudes, and behaviors (that are defined by our organizational role and responsibilities)? Brands are greater than the sum of their parts—and so too are customers.

Why Invest in Brands?

Companies investing in brand building basically have three simple reasons for doing so: to drive customer loyalty, to maintain price premium, or to increase revenue growth. The real challenge is not just building great brands that drive revenue growth and loyalty, but building them at a lower cost and faster than your competition!

Branding Rationale

The traditional thinking around branding was to endow a product or service with unique characteristics through the creative use of name, slogan, packaging, and advertising. In a world where there is a muddle of images and messages, however, it is increasingly difficult for a brand to rise above the noise to be noticed and remembered. A more sophisticated and strategic concept of branding is needed. The rationale behind branding is all about creating differentiation.

Differentiation leads to positive discrimination, and large or at least profitable brand share. Brand marketers must deliver tangibles and/or intangibles that differentiate a brand. This differentiation not only needs to be perceived but also valued.

It is logical to assume that the main objective of branding is to create high-involvement situations. If the branding exercise fails to deliver a relevant and valued differentiation to its targeted involvement segments, then are its efforts unsuccessful?

Strategic Considerations

If consumers are not prepared to pay for differentiating activity by way of perceiving or appreciating any unique qualities between brands, there will be no economic justification for branding exercises. In any product category, if differences are not valued, buyers tend to discriminate between brands on the sole basis of price and availability.

The question is:
Does it really make sense to invest in building brands in low-involvement markets?

Or, is it even possible to generate high brand involvement in the face of low category involvement?

A good branding strategist is capable of completely transforming categories to create new categories or sub-categories.

Says nothing about me ...

... Says a lot about me now.

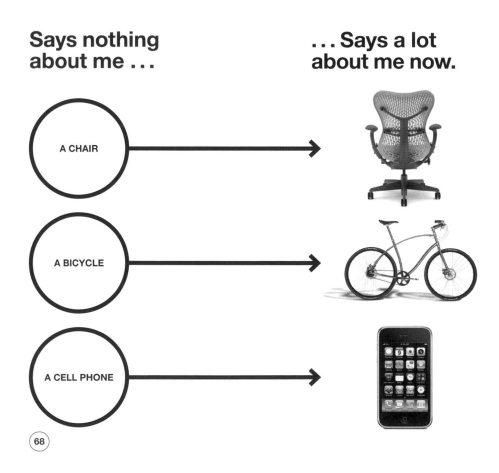

A CHAIR

A BICYCLE

A CELL PHONE

Personal diaries were probably not considered "expressive" until the advent of the Filofax brand. Similarly, owning a TV might be considered low in self-expression, but an iPhone makes a statement. Other examples include Apple's iMac, Herman Miller's Aeron chair, a Burberry raincoat, a Louis Vuitton bag or an Aston Martin. While credit cards and fine writing instruments were once status symbols, "expressive" items are now replaced by personal electronic gadgets like iPhones and BlackBerries.

Says a lot
about me ...

... Says less
about me now.

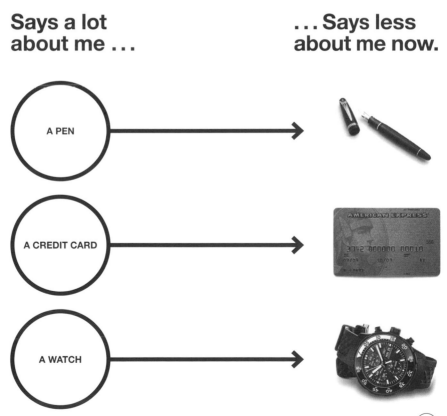

A PEN

A CREDIT CARD

A WATCH

Brand personalities help firms differentiate their products from the competition and build brand equity (value).

"Stand for something or you'll fall for anything!"

Consumers don't buy products, they buy the personalities associated with those products. Big K cola and Coke are equal in taste tests ... but not in market share.

Consumers don't buy on taste alone. Brand personalities help consumers define their own self concepts and express their identities to others. People find meaning only through those brands with personalities, not from products.

The Involvement Grid

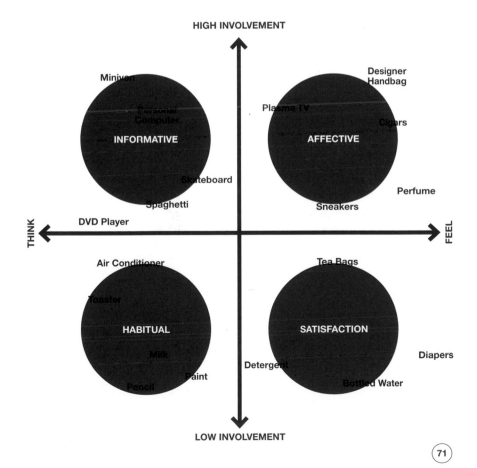

HIGH INVOLVEMENT

Minivan

Personal Computer

INFORMATIVE

Skateboard

Spaghetti

DVD Player

Designer Handbag

Plasma TV

Cigars

AFFECTIVE

Perfume

Sneakers

THINK

FEEL

Air Conditioner

Toaster

HABITUAL

Milk

Paint

Pencil

Tea Bags

SATISFACTION

Diapers

Detergent

Bottled Water

LOW INVOLVEMENT

Advertising and Branding

Brand management has been taking place for years without a unified theory. Common sense branding is widely practiced. There are fundamental questions about its underlying principles. Many equate great creative ideas and advertising campaigns to successful brand building.

The romanticized view of advertising is that it can change what people think about your brand. Advertising does not change what people think about your brand (which is always difficult). It only has them think about your brand.

Despite a recent boom in articles and books on the subject, branding remains an art. There are unrealistic expectations that methodologies or approaches are out there that can consistently, repetitively, or systematically create great brands. We have solved only one-third of the brand puzzle.

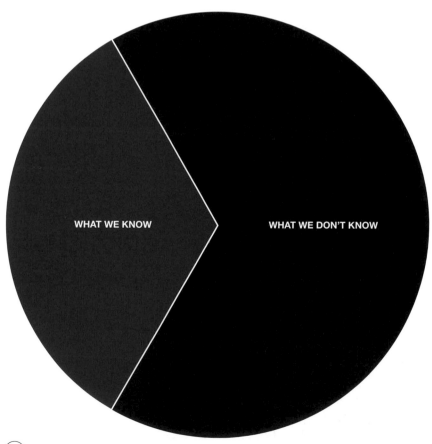

WHAT WE KNOW

WHAT WE DON'T KNOW

What More Can Be Branded?

Companies have been successful in branding bricks, paper, chickens, diamonds, milk, salt, sugar, oranges, bananas, microprocessors, and even air, water, and sand. Universities, cities, charities, and celebrities have been successful in branding their cultures, causes, streets, and styles. And while the no-brand or anti-brand movement has successfully made its point, we all know that no logo is still some brand.

So how much is too much? Is there a saturation point at which we're sopping wet from too much branding, a tipping point where we fall into the abyss of advertising and product identification?

Maybe. Probably not. Actually, only if and when the best brands cease to engage consumers on levels of symbolic and social interaction.

The Brand as a Sign

Social and symbolic interaction begins at the level of the sign. Like a sign, a brand doesn't exist within the global system of brands except by opposition to and difference from other brands: you need your own signifier (Swoosh) and signified (victory) to make your brand (Nike) part of the consumer lexicon. Without differentiation, you're not communicating anything of substance to consumers. Without substance, they won't have any reason to care about you, anything to say about you and, most importantly, any reason to make your brand come to life between themselves.

This is the business case for brands. It's both limited and limiting. It suggests that brands exist in a closed system inhabited only by products, their creators, and managers. For an anthropologist, like the sign, it is a communicative tool that helps people choreograph consumption, facilitate the flow of social relations, and identify the value and appropriateness of our relationships with each other.

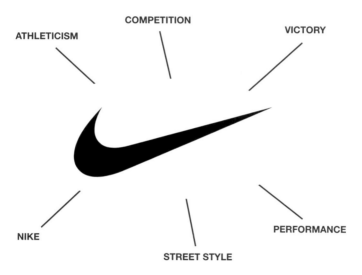

COMPETITION

ATHLETICISM

VICTORY

NIKE

STREET STYLE

PERFORMANCE

"The brand is a set of relations between products in time." —Celia Lury, *Brands: The Logos of the Global Economy*

Brand Customer Interactions and Relationships Matrix

FREQUENT BRAND–
CUSTOMER INTERACTION

CLOSE BRAND–CUSTOMER RELATIONSHIP

DISTANT BRAND–CUSTOMER RELATIONSHIP

Brand maintenance efforts are required to sustain the overall brand presence. Event-driven interactions occur only during a short and intense period of time. Examples: Real Estate Agents, Car Dealers, Funeral Homes, Private Bankers, Cosmetic Surgeons, etc.

Brand building consists mainly of mass media advertising, point-of-sale, and packaging. Customer seldom needs to have contact with brand owner. Channel partners control most of the customer experience. Most fast moving consumer products belong to this quadrant.

Brand building is mostly driven by customer experience. Internal branding is vital and operationalization of the brand will need to be allocated with considerable resources. The resulting impact can be sustaining and build strong competitive barriers. Examples: Hotels, Airlines, Retail Banking, Retailing, Restaurants, etc.

Brand building impact is vastly influenced by the frequent interactions with customers by front line employees. A lot of marketing automation is done through call center and the Internet due to economic reasons. Examples: Credit Cards, Utilities, Mail Order Merchants, Cable TV, etc.

INFREQUENT BRAND–
CUSTOMER INTERACTION

75

Why do we need a theory for strategic brand management?

Because theory is eminently practical. Managers are the world's most voracious consumers of theories. Every time a brand marketing decision is made, it is usually based on some implicit understanding of what causes what and why. The real problem is that they often use a one-size-fits-all theory. There are many ways to build great brands. Here are the four basic approaches:

01 Planning
02 Imagery
03 Customer Experience
04 Self-Expression

Branding by Planning
Procter & Gamble
Pepsi
Intel
Gillette
Nestlé
GM

Branding by Imagery
Abercrombie & Fitch
Calvin Klein
American Apparel
BMW
Absolut
Milk
Tag Heuer

**Branding
by Customer
Experience**
Starbucks
Zappos
Southwest Airlines
Hertz
Disney
Marriott
Apple

**Branding by
Self-Expression**
Louis Vuitton
Gap
Prada
Swatch
Method
Mini
Allsteel

Branding by Planning

Here branding is approached as part of a formal strategic planning process. Most of the time this occurs in the context of strategic marketing planning. The typical approach uses portfolio and product life cycle concepts together with overall market overviews and competitive intelligence. The information is distilled and analyzed through each individual brand's performance in terms of market share and margin contribution. The heart of the exercise is positioning to ensure that products cover all necessary profitable or emerging segments and use brand to achieve these objectives. Usually, multi-brand organizations and category managers assume the ownership role of the brand portfolio and manage the brand architecture. The key is to articulate the overall brand strategy and approach (e.g., a master brand approach using targeted sub-brands). This entails far more than just organizing the brands as individual performers. To truly optimize their value requires a dynamic framework that makes the most of their interrelationships under a system of brands working together to drive clarity in the marketplace and increase synergy and leverage within the company's portfolio.

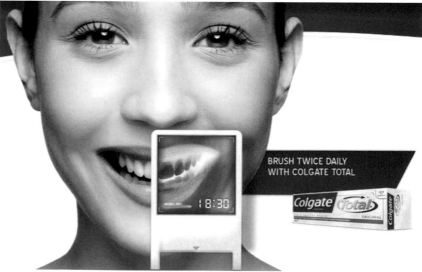

Branding by Imagery

Here branding is approached in a more functional manner. Usually advertising agencies take a leading role and advertising is linked to branding. The levers of brand building consist mainly of TV commercials, posters, and print advertisements.

In some cases, a first showing of a 60-second TV spot during the Super Bowl is a milestone of the brand building effort. Visually stunning posters and ads in national magazines such as *Vogue* or *Vanity Fair* are also used. Marketers and agencies closely link the brand to creative advertising execution.

Sometimes the burden is given to a celebrated photographer. The Calvin Klein success is hugely indebted to Bruce Weber, and Benetton to Oliver Toscani. These photographers gave those brands meaning.

The risk here is that advertising failure means brand failure. But a great campaign produces a very desirable brand and many products and advertising agencies came to fame with just one highly memorable campaign. The marketer continues to enjoy the benefits for years.

Branding by Customer Experience

Companies see customers taking functional benefits, a high-quality product, and a positive brand image as a given. What they want is products, services, and marketing communications that dazzle their senses, touch their hearts, and stimulate their minds. Here the customer becomes the most important part of the brand. Over the years many brands have transformed themselves into experience brands by creating a compelling customer experience.

Starbucks and The Body Shop did not use mass advertising to build brands. Instead, they put their resources into designing and delivering unique experiences. The Tiffany & Co. experience consists not only of the purchase experience, but also the whole experience of giving and receiving something special. The Tiffany & Co. trademark is inseparably linked to the ageless elegance and quality that define the brand. The blue box serves as an identifier and sensory reminder of this, as does the Hermès online experience by relentlessly improving user experiences.

Branding by Self-Expression

Here companies put the role of brand building partially into the hands of customers. This has long been practiced by the luxury and sporting goods industries as well as the fashion industry, where there's never enough time to build a relevant and meaningful brand that keeps pace with fast-changing customer needs. Consumers in these categories do not want to use the brand to endorse or reflect their personality; rather it contributes to building a personal or individual brand. In other words, strong brand identities deter customers because they dominate. The consumer uses the brand as a tool or status symbol, then adds in his or her own hallmark to express who they are, who they want others to think they are, and how they see the world and things. The brand only requires some associated meaning so customers can pick, or mix and match with other values or uses they identify with as part of building their "Me" brand. Consumers actively participate in creating meanings for brands.

Sometimes, they do more than actively participate. By transforming basic products into complex signifiers of identity, performance, and social membership, consumers often oversee some of the finer details of how a brand is "managed" in the real world.

With help from Marlon Brando to Dee Dee Ramone to the kids they stood for, work wear, first sewn up in 19th-century San Francisco and then ripped around the world, became the global signifier of youth culture.

Thanks to early B-boys in Baltimore, Philadelphia, and New York City, a 1982 basketball sneaker with no advertising or marketing budget became an enduring icon of global hip hop culture.

And with Portland bike messengers latching on to its underdog status and bar discounts, a down-and-out beer became a celebration of American low-brow culture.

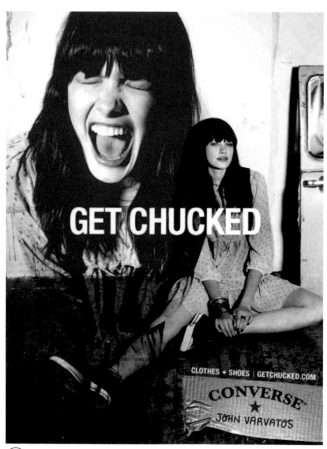

Brand success is a case of more than meets the eye. That Pabst Blue Ribbon has enjoyed increasing sales in a dwindling beer market since 2002, Nike's Air Force 1 has been remastered and sold out in more design manifestations than any product and, although the last few years haven't been kind, Levi's 501s have been a fashion staple for more than 50 years is testament to what it is that transforms products into brands:

Usability
Does it work for me, work well, and fit into my life?

Consumability
Does it taste good? Look good? Feel good?

Performativity
Does it help do/say/be/show something important?

Desirability
Is there a social, cultural, or personal need it fulfills?

Of these, desirability is where branding usually enters the picture. But in the case of Pabst Blue Ribbon, Nike's Air Force 1, and Levi's jeans, branding didn't enter the picture until well into the success curve of these brands. One day, maybe after fumbling through sales reports, someone in an office woke up to the fact that kids on the street made these brands hot, not Brand Managers or media.

Does that mean I can't architect consumer attraction to my brand?

No. What it means is that consumer cultures and communities are often best left to their own devices to build themselves from the ground up with their own rules and regulations. With a little field exploration to determine the boundaries that these cultures and communities wish to keep, permeate, or dissolve between you and them—and with a healthy respect for those boundaries should you want to maintain your most loyal consumer base—you might collaborate, nurture, or simply help perpetuate the conditions under which they will continue to thrive.

4

26

58

37

04
Managing Brand Value

People often confuse a new name or logo with branding

Many companies have been led to believe that if they get a new brand name, logo, and marketing materials, they've solved the branding problem. This is the number one mistake most companies make when it comes to branding. This is a costly proposition, and the end result may not produce meaningful changes to the bottom line.

People often confuse corporate identity with corporate branding

The "corporate identity" approach is preferred by design firms in the business of logo and brand name development, letterhead design, stationery and business forms, uniforms, shop interiors, and so on. However, brand name and logo are not the most important part of corporate branding. What really matters is what the brand name and logo stand for, the trust they have earned (and will earn) with customers. We should all aspire to build trusted brands because they retain loyal customers for years—or even a lifetime.

According to Wharton Professor J. Reibstein, the actual name of a company doesn't make much of a difference. What companies end up doing is a significant amount of advertising and creating an image around the name.

If a company wants to be regarded in a certain way (brand identity), everything must support that desired identity.

Does the corporate/business strategy and the company's execution against it support that desired identity? If so, then the desired brand identity may be appropriate (obviously, there are a lot of other considerations). If not, the brand identity will not be attainable until alignment is achieved.

Alternatively, it's appropriate to use the desired brand identity as an "end state" for company management and employees to visualize, to drive change and support the corporate strategy. Establish a strategic process to allow your company to realize that vision over time. The company strategy and brand strategy grow together toward a common direction.

Start with Brand Strategy or Business Strategy?

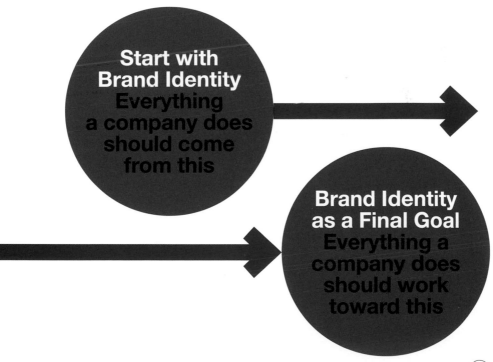

Start with
Brand Identity
Everything
a company does
should come
from this

Brand Identity
as a Final Goal
Everything a
company does
should work
toward this

If a brand does not have vital consumer meaning, then it is not worthwhile investing financially and organizationally in its leadership. It is not worth the time and resources to push it or to make it a rallying point for the skills of the company's people; nor is it worthwhile living the value relationships that emerge from the branding process.

Conversely, if a brand does have vital (and self-perpetuating) consumer meaning, companies discover that there are more significant similarities than differences among consumers in their sphere of business as they market a brand's essence around the world.

Rowntree failed to recognize that an impulse-grabbing concept like "have a break, have a Kit Kat" could capture consumer imagination and establish a global and local "time-out" place in consumer lives. But Nestlé did. Appreciating that Rowntree's leading brands had enough meaning invested in them to be worthwhile, they purchased the company. More than just a US$4.5 billion value (based on past performance), Nestlé's 1988 acquisition of Rowntree was about the future advantages that could be conjured from the latent essences and meanings of its brands.

Al Ries and Jack Trout wrote that "owning a word in the prospect's mind" is the most powerful concept. This occurs when the association is so strong that any word is immediately linked to a brand. They insisted that "no matter how complicated the product, no matter how complicated the needs of the market, it's always better to focus on one word or benefit rather than two or three."

This is often true of a single product or category brand, but today's brands have become very sophisticated. Owning category words and benefit-related words are not enough. Competitors will try to undermine this association. Instead, own values beyond the narrow focus of functional benefits. Benefit-related word association is less powerful when quality, service, and design are at par and companies aggressively expand their product range targeting different segments. Mercedes owns the word *engineering*, BMW *performance*, and Volvo *safety*. Yet when Mercedes launched the C-series to appeal to younger segments, BMW launched the 7 series for those who appreciate state-of-the-art engineering, and Volvo revamped its product range with a sportier look to suggest speed, those associations quickly became meaningless.

Brands with lower brand meaning simply cannot support many extensions. For brand extensions, answer these questions:

— **Is the extension consistent with your longer-term brand vision?**

— **Does the extension actually add value to your brand?**

— **Are you able to deliver on the branded customer experience?**

— **Is the benefit consistent with your positioning?**

— **If this extension fails, is it a major or minor setback for your brand?**

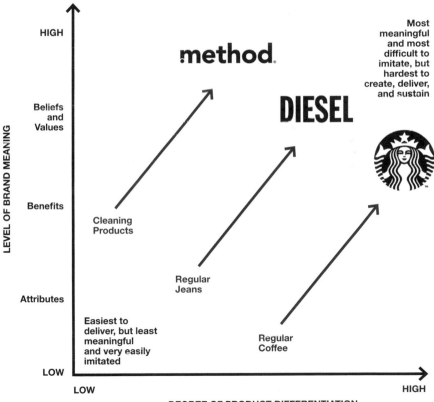

What is the difference between a brand promise and a mission statement?

The basic difference is one of perspective. A mission statement generally articulates an organization's internal perspective regarding direction and objectives. On the other hand, the brand promise is written primarily from the customers' perspective, articulating the essence of the brand's benefits (functional and emotional) experienced through a brand's products and services.

Value's Elusive Meaning

Value is a simple word with a complex meaning. Value is defined in the mind of the customer. Yet value is neither a constant nor even a consistent impression. Value depends both on situation and context. A customer's perception of value can and usually does change with time and circumstances, often unpredictably. Certain attributes of a product or service may be valued while others are not— some features may be valued negatively. Alternatives affect value perceptions, and choices are constantly expanding. Changing needs affect value perceptions, but those needs constantly change too. In spite of the volatility of value's meaning, most of the time people form relatively stable perceptions of a brand's image, reputation, and value promise. Brand marketing's role is to bring the two together.

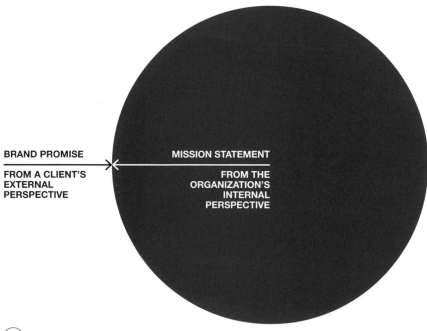

BRAND PROMISE

MISSION STATEMENT

FROM A CLIENT'S
EXTERNAL
PERSPECTIVE

FROM THE
ORGANIZATION'S
INTERNAL
PERSPECTIVE

Brand Awareness Is Not the Same as Brand Differentiation

Despite the lip service paid to developing brand strategies and investing in branding efforts, many brands are still moving toward commoditization. They are becoming much more well-known and yet less differentiated in the minds of consumers. You must ask yourself these questions before you invest heavily in building your brand:

01 What is the level of achievable brand differentiation in your category or industry?

02 Do you have a sound growth plan as well as a growth mind-set in place to capitalize on your brand equity as a result of your brand investment?

03 How will your existing customers respond to your increased commoditization?

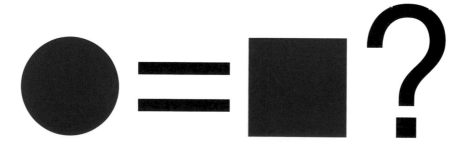

Price Is More Important Than Brand

Online Bookstore amazon.com

Rental Car Hertz

Office Supply Store STAPLES

Bookstore BARNES&NOBLE

Bottled Water evian

Gas Station Mobil

Long Distance Telephone Provider Sprint

Cellular Phone Provider AT&T

Brand Is More Important Than Price

Beer

Liquor

Automobile

Cola TAB

Personal Computer

Brokerage Charles Schwab

Major Household Appliance

Motor Oil

Many consumers tell researchers that they are perfectly happy with the brands they are using, yet jump at the next opportunity to switch brands. Brand awareness and satisfaction are poor predictors of human behavior and we should not be putting too much emphasis on them.

Loyalty has two different meanings: Loyalty due to a lack of choice or pure convenience versus loyalty as a result of commitment

I am with you because I really love you.

(YOU ARE THE ONLY ONE)

I am with you because you are convenient.

(THERE WAS NO ONE ELSE)

Brand Metrics

Metrics provide direction, not control. They monitor progress to success to prevent firms from driving blindfolded.

Metric	Measured by
Relative Satisfaction	Consumer preference or satisfaction as percent average for market or competitors
Salience	Relative market awareness
Commitment	Index of switchability (or similar measure of retention, loyalty, purchase intent, or relationship bonding)
Relative Perceived Quality	Perceived quality satisfaction as average percent of market or against competitors
Relative Price	Market share (value) or market share (volume)
Availability	Distribution (e.g., weighted percent of retail outlets carrying the brand)

Market Leader = Loyalty Leader?

If not, then you need to decide which one is your Prime Branding Objective.

In a recent worldwide survey, Young & Rubicam surveyed 30,000 consumers and 6,000 brands and found that the way to build brand equity was to focus on differentiation, not awareness. Their research found that the traditional F.R.E.D. (familiarity, relevance, esteem, and differentiation) approach to marketing was not as effective as a strategy that emphasized developing product differentiation over awareness.

Product Category	Market Leader's Loyalty Rate	Brand Loyalty Leader Rate
High Loyalty Rates:		
Cigarettes	Marlboro (42)	Tareyton (74)
Cold Remedies	Contac (38)	Bayer DCT (50)
Headache Remedies	Bayer (33)	Tylenol (45)
Medium Loyalty Rates:		
Toothpaste	Crest (38)	Ultrabrite (39)
Cooking Oil	Crisco (36)	Mazola (39)
Cola	Coca-Cola (29)	Tab (43)
Low Loyalty Rates:		
Facial Tissues	Kleenex (18)	Puffs (28)
Paper Towels	Bounty (17)	Brawny (22)
Aluminum	Reynolds (17)	No-name (17)

SOURCE: DON JOHNSON, 'A RE-EXAMINATION OF THE PROCESS OF BRANDING,' HARVARD BUSINESS SCHOOL

Who's Winning?

MARKET LEADER → CONSUMER

CONSUMER → LOYALTY LEADER
CONSUMER → LOYALTY LEADER
CONSUMER → LOYALTY LEADER

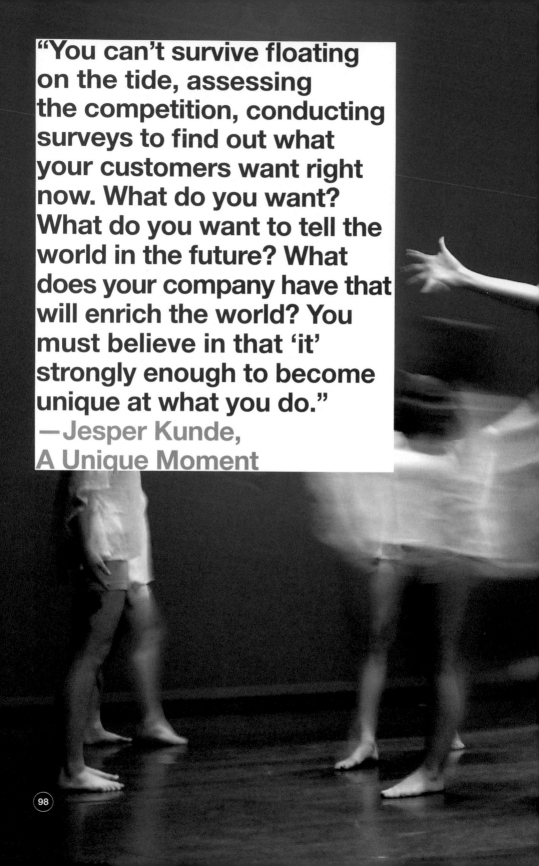

"You can't survive floating on the tide, assessing the competition, conducting surveys to find out what your customers want right now. What do you want? What do you want to tell the world in the future? What does your company have that will enrich the world? You must believe in that 'it' strongly enough to become unique at what you do."
—Jesper Kunde,
A Unique Moment

Believe in your "it"

99

As product spaces become modularized, componentized, and compartmentalized to address the individual, customized targeted needs of markets, the correspondent market space, and the value chains in them become more integrated.

In a sense, products disintegrate while markets become integrated. This is forced onto ever more expansive value chains.

Individual Products

Integrated Markets

The colonization of physical space is now extending to the mental space and happening at an even faster pace.

Companies used to be *product producers*

Now they must become *meaning brokers*

"WHO ARE YOU [these days]?" and WHAT can you do for me? —Tom Peters, Management Guru

Innovation alone does not create value. It simply offers design and engineering feats, not things that excite real people. The true innovator's dilemma is how to build brands that create barriers for competition as innovative products or technologies become commoditized. Innovation alone is not the answer.

You must get beyond innovation. You must make the connection between innovation and customer value. The connection is made through the brand.

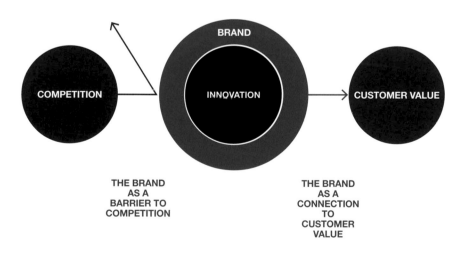

COMPETITION

BRAND

INNOVATION

CUSTOMER VALUE

THE BRAND
AS A
BARRIER TO
COMPETITION

THE BRAND
AS A
CONNECTION
TO
CUSTOMER
VALUE

"The idea that business is just a numbers affair has always struck me as preposterous. For one thing, I've never been particularly good at numbers, but I think I've done a reasonable job with feelings. And I'm convinced that it is feelings—and feelings alone—that account for the success of the Virgin brand in all of its myriad forms."
—Sir Richard Branson, Virgin Group

If you want to build a company that sustains growth and shareholder value, would you rather your CEO was a Chief Emotions Officer or a Chief Numbers Officer?

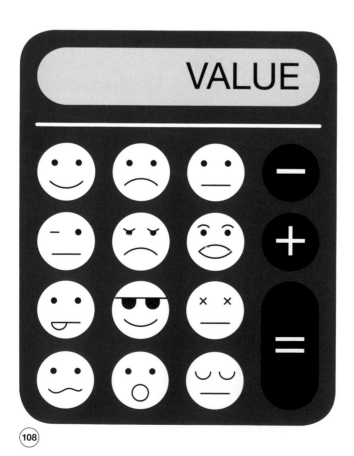

"As chairman and CEO, my job is to provide a corporate structure and culture that enables our cast members to perpetuate the values and traditions that fuel the Disney magic ... I am, in effect, the chief brand manager."

"I take my responsibility as a steward of the brand very seriously: to protect it, enhance it and try to ensure that it is even more valuable and beloved in the 21st century than it was in the 20th. It's a responsibility I share with all 120,000 Disney cast members around the world. We all know that the Disney brand is our most valuable asset."

—Michael Eisner, Disney

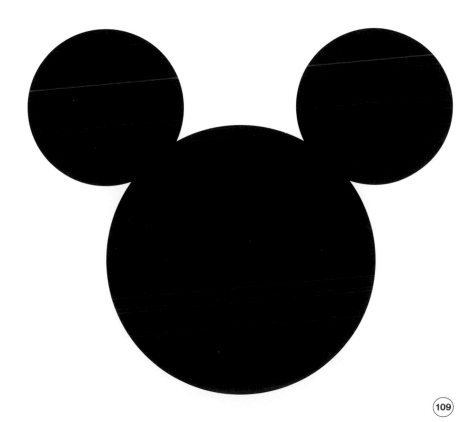

COMPANIES WILL THRIVE ON THE BASIS OF THEIR STORIES AND MYTHS

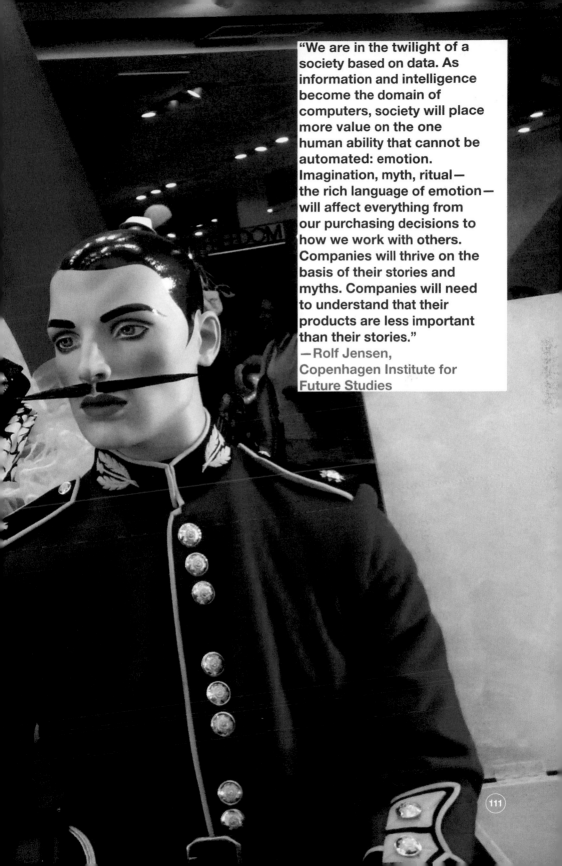

"We are in the twilight of a society based on data. As information and intelligence become the domain of computers, society will place more value on the one human ability that cannot be automated: emotion. Imagination, myth, ritual— the rich language of emotion— will affect everything from our purchasing decisions to how we work with others. Companies will thrive on the basis of their stories and myths. Companies will need to understand that their products are less important than their stories."
—Rolf Jensen, Copenhagen Institute for Future Studies

111

True
Loyalty Is
About
Commitment

112

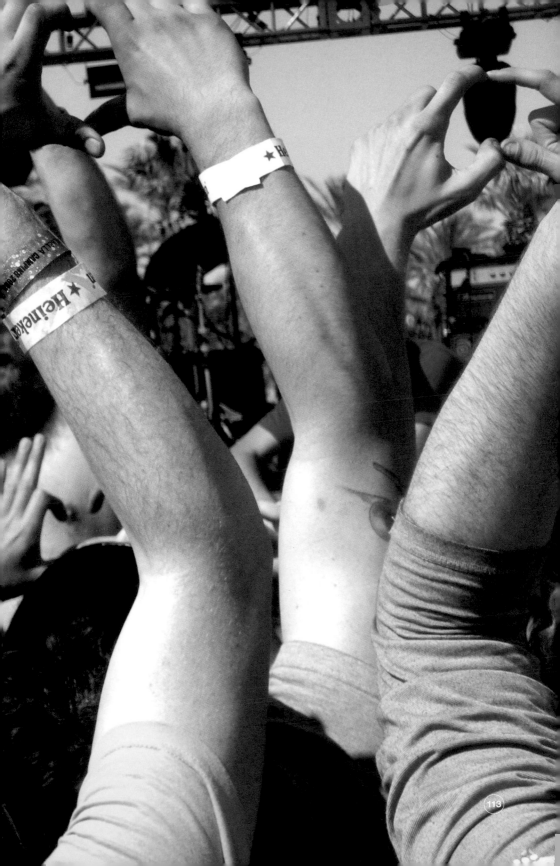

"A great brand taps into emotions. Emotions drive most, if not all, of our decisions. A brand reaches out with a powerful connecting experience. It's an emotional connecting point that transcends the product."
—Scott Bedbury, Nike, Starbucks

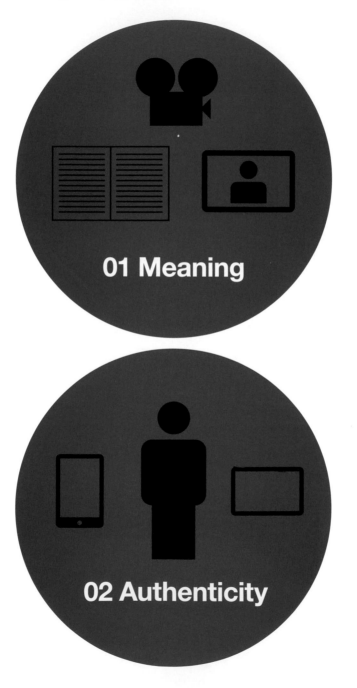

01 Meaning

02 Authenticity

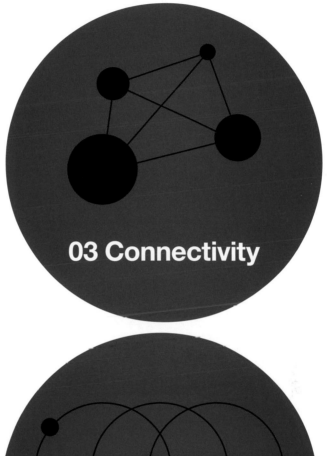

03 Connectivity

04 Relevancy

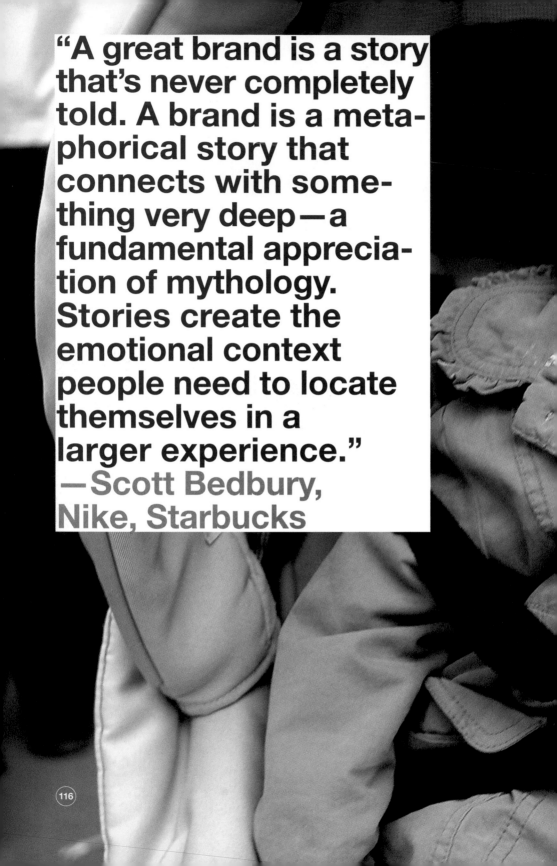

"A great brand is a story that's never completely told. A brand is a meta-phorical story that connects with some-thing very deep—a fundamental apprecia-tion of mythology. Stories create the emotional context people need to locate themselves in a larger experience."
—Scott Bedbury, Nike, Starbucks

Once upon a Time...

VERY
IMPORTANT:
THE STORY
NEVER ENDS

"Most executives have no idea how to add value to a market in the metaphysical world. But that is what the market will cry out for in the future. There is no lack of 'physical' products to choose between." —Jesper Kunde, *A Unique Moment* [on the excellence of Nokia, Nike, Lego, Virgin et al.]

PRODUCTS IN
THE PHYSICAL WORLD

PRODUCTS IN
THE METAPHYSICAL WORLD

119

What more can you do to today's consumers' already battered brain? More new products, more new services, more outbound direct marketing phone calls during dinner time, and more stress? If others are selling stress, then the market is need of products that heal.

How about the marketer as meta-physician and the brand as prescription?

What's Your Healing Benefit?

The new reality for marketers is that only those offerings that go beyond the need for superior product quality, competitive pricing, and emotionally driven image-building communications to deliver some healing benefit beyond the functional purpose of the product itself will have enough consumer appeal to break through the defense. This will be a new competitive dimension. From recycled to sustainable to CSR and beyond, doing good unto ourselves, our consumers and others will differentiate the past from the new present, the leaders from the followers.

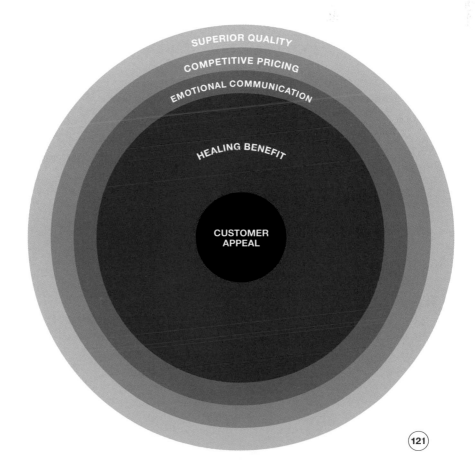

SUPERIOR QUALITY

COMPETITIVE PRICING

EMOTIONAL COMMUNICATION

HEALING BENEFIT

CUSTOMER APPEAL

Swiss Chocolate Knife

Swiss Chocolate Knife

Swiss
Chocolate Knife
gefüllt mit Haselnuss-Gianduja
filled with hazelnut praliné

The Challenge

How can you address and fulfill the consumer's deepest needs and wants—particularly if you're not in the pharma, cosmetics, or entertainment industry?

It involves the deepest understanding of what the consumer cares most about and what state of mind they're in. At the heart of an effective brand strategy philosophy is the belief that nothing is so powerful as an insight into human nature, what compulsions drive consumers, what instincts inform their actions and how they perform—even though language so often camouflages real motivations.

01
If your thinking is locked in a database, break out of it!
Numbers can be a prison. They reveal patterns, not people. Instead, develop a culture with an insatiable appetite for qualitative research.

03
Prioritize what people DO over what they SAY.
Interviews are good, but the most valuable answers are in the consumer's actions. How they reflect, refute, or reveal layers of articulated and unarticulated need and desire leads to the deepest insights.

02
Turn your focus groups into fieldwork.
No amount of coffee, donuts, and cash-on-completion to taste chocolate bars or describe shopping patterns will mine the kind of critical, deep insights you need. Stop creating and controlling the context in which you learn about your consumer.

The Solution

In the space between brands and consumers exists a complex web of personal, social, and cultural relationships, perceptions, meanings, actions, reactions, and interactions. Understanding that web and, more importantly, appreciating and celebrating it for its complexity—and for how every little vibration across it could signal impending doom for your brand—is absolutely key to cultivating authentic, dynamic relationships with consumers. So how do you do that? By nurturing a brand culture that is intensely critical, introspective, and research centric. Here are five ways to get that culture started.

04

Mash up your staff.

Send brand managers out into the field with consumer insights, designers with usability, and strategists with marketing. When a culture of collaborative research is part of every job description, every job will contribute to furthering that culture.

05

Stop believing your own hype.

No amount of office mythology or self-congratulations can disguise what you ARE NOT. If consumers are saying it, it's probably true. Now is the time to start engaging them on their terms and in their language to discover the path forward.

59

18

03

126

05
Brand
Leadership

Brand Management versus Brand Leadership

There are basically two different orientations toward brand: as images and as promises. It's not surprising that there are two fundamentally different approaches to brand development as well. These two approaches, brand management and brand leadership, are codified by David Aaker and differ in a variety of ways.

Brand management focuses on the short-term. Its primary tool is promotion. Brand managers never have enough money and seldom have true control over the dollars they do have. Brand leadership is about the long-term. Brand leaders understand that building brand equity takes time, money, and talent. They know that a successful brand is not built in one budget year or one product launch. Brand leadership is based on the premise that brand building not only creates brand equity, but is also necessary for institutional success. With brand leadership, the institution's most senior leaders recognize that building the brand results in a competitive advantage that pays financially.

Brand management is tactical, visual, and reactive. It's preoccupied with the 3 Ls of branding: look, letterhead, and logo. Brand leadership is visionary and promise-driven. It concentrates on building brand value that translates into loyalty and market power. Metrics are in place to measure progress. The goal is brand equity.

Brand management and brand leadership represent two ends of a vast continuum. For many marketers, brand leadership might initially be out of reach and exists only on the company's annual report. Their quickest gains might actually be generated by a consistent brand management strategy. To build a brand promise that consumers will value and, in doing so, help build brand equity, it is essential for everyone in that continuum to understand the progression of branding from management to leadership.

Category	Brand Management	Brand Leadership
Focus	Limited	Broad
Product/market scope	Single products/markets	Multiple products and markets
Brand structures	Simple	Complex brand architectures
Number of brands	Focus on single brands	Category focus multiple brands
Country scope	Single country	Global or national perspective
Communication focus	External customer only	Internal as well as external

**The Five Brand
Leadership Benchmarks:
As you look at these
five brand stages, note how
they are tiered. You need
to firmly establish one before
you can move on to the next.**

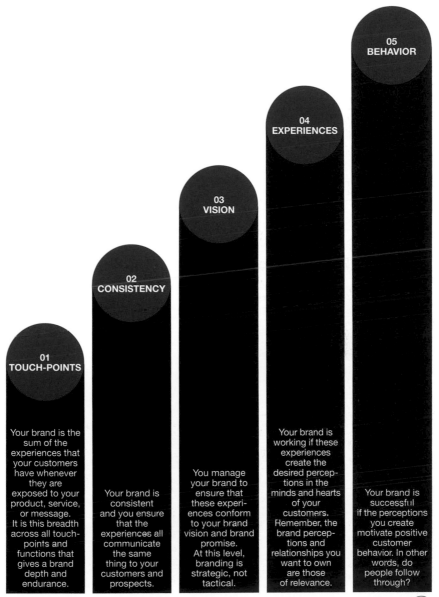

**05
BEHAVIOR**

**04
EXPERIENCES**

**03
VISION**

**02
CONSISTENCY**

**01
TOUCH-POINTS**

Your brand is the sum of the experiences that your customers have whenever they are exposed to your product, service, or message. It is this breadth across all touch-points and functions that gives a brand depth and endurance.

Your brand is consistent and you ensure that the experiences all communicate the same thing to your customers and prospects.

You manage your brand to ensure that these experiences conform to your brand vision and brand promise. At this level, branding is strategic, not tactical.

Your brand is working if these experiences create the desired perceptions in the minds and hearts of your customers. Remember, the brand perceptions and relationships you want to own are those of relevance.

Your brand is successful if the perceptions you create motivate positive customer behavior. In other words, do people follow through?

Creating a clear brand architecture to help structure position for today and tomorrow helps build that brand by ensuring everyone within an organization works to a common and clearly understood goal.

P&G and PepsiCo have hundreds, GM has 8 brand names, BMW has 3, IBM has 2, and Starbucks and Apple have 1. Between mergers and acquisitions, aggressive brand extensions, and the increasing complexities of sub-brands, endorsed brands, and co-brands, it gets more and more complicated. Often the task includes a periodic regrouping of multiple product groups and brand families, repositioning them to reflect their role in the market and to create a structure for immediate success. Establishing a clear and coherent brand architecture creates structure within which vital day-to-day tactical decisions can be made. Without this brand architecture in place, these tactical decisions become strategic and long-winded in nature.

Brand architecture is the logical, strategic, and relational structure for all of the brands in the organization's brand portfolio. The objective is to maximize clarity, synergy, and leverage to maximize customer value and internal efficiencies.

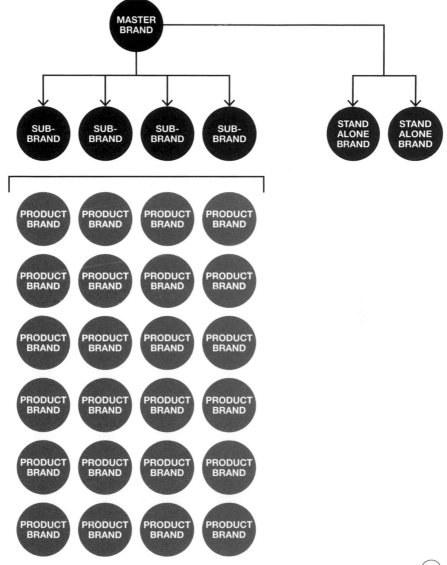

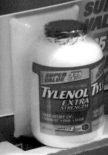

Understanding Brand Architecture

Advantages of developing a brand architecture:

01 It helps everyone in the organization see and understand all the connections between corporate brands, sub-brands, and master brands.

02 It simplifies decision making when it comes to allocating and sharing marketing resources such as advertising and promotions.

03 It protects brands from becoming over-leveraged and diluted by over-extending communications messages and graphic design options.

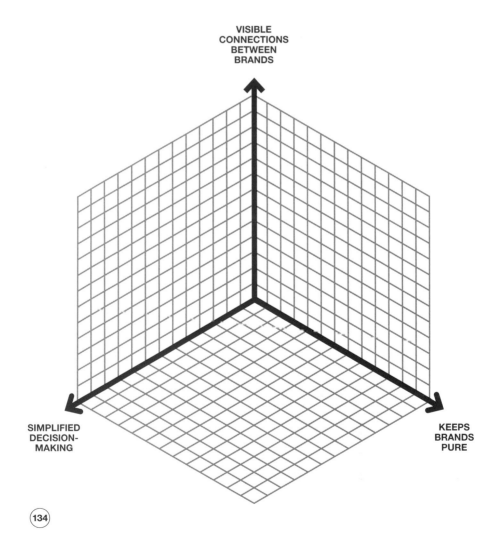

VISIBLE
CONNECTIONS
BETWEEN
BRANDS

SIMPLIFIED
DECISION-
MAKING

KEEPS
BRANDS
PURE

P&G's brand architecture effectively manages the relationships between product, brands, and market segments. Head & Shoulders dominates the dandruff control shampoo category and Pert Plus targets the market for combined shampoo and conditioner. Pantene is positioned as a brand with a technological heritage and the power to enhance hair vitality. These three brands optimize their brand coverage by not being merchandised under a P&G product brand name. The lesson? Avoid a brand association that is incompatible with another offering and may adversely affect its performance.

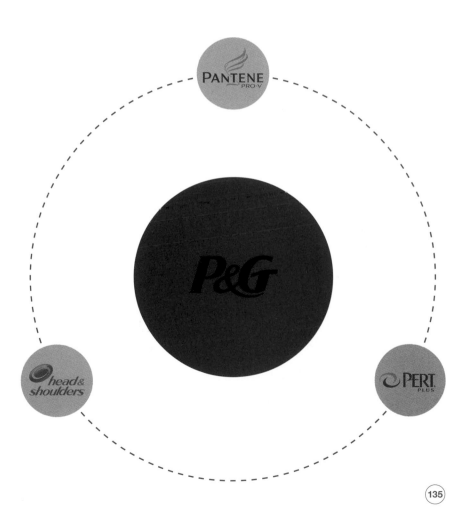

Understanding Brand Architecture

It is very difficult to offer a generalization on how to put a vast number of brands in categories and wed sets of them and their relationships into a composite brand architecture. Each industry and category context is different, as are corporate views. The tendency is toward having a master brand. Only when there is a compelling need (and a budget) should a separate brand be considered. The big question is: can the business support a new brand?

The needs usually consist of one or more of the following:

01 Create and own a different set of associations

02 Develop a totally new product offering or a category

03 Avoid conflict in brand association and identities

04 Avoid channel conflict

05 Create a price-driven label for competitive reasons

06 Fulfill needs for new geographies or unique customer segments

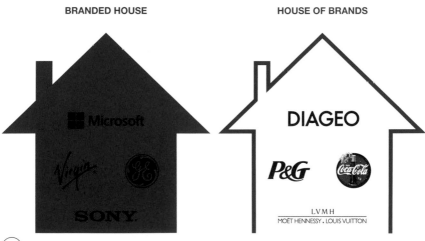

BRANDED HOUSE

HOUSE OF BRANDS

Case Study:
Branded House
versus
House of Brands

GENERAL ELECTRIC: BRANDED HOUSE	PROCTER & GAMBLE: A HOUSE OF BRANDS

 GE Lighting

 GE Transportation

 GE Money

 GE Commercial Finance

 GE Appliances

 GE Energy

 GE Water & Process Technologies

 GE Healthcare

 GE Commercial Aviation Services

 GE Oil & Gas

 Lumination

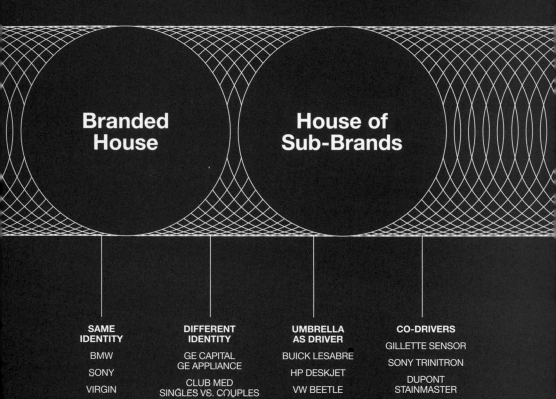

SAME IDENTITY	DIFFERENT IDENTITY	UMBRELLA AS DRIVER	CO-DRIVERS
BMW	GE CAPITAL	BUICK LESABRE	GILLETTE SENSOR
SONY	GE APPLIANCE	HP DESKJET	SONY TRINITRON
VIRGIN	CLUB MED SINGLES VS. COUPLES	VW BEETLE	DUPONT STAINMASTER
	LEVI—EUROPE LEVI—U.S.A.		

Endorsed House of Brands

House of Brands

STRONG ENDORSEMENT	LINKED NAME	TOKEN ENDORSEMENT	SHADOW ENDORSER	NOT CONNECTED
COURTYARD BY MARRIOTT	DKNY	GRAPE-NUTS FROM POST	TIDE (P&G)	THOMSON (GE)
OBSESSION BY CALVIN KLEIN	McMUFFIN	SONY PLAYSTATION	LEXUS (TOYOTA)	SATURN (GM)
FRIENDS & FAMILY BY MCI	NESTEA	DOCKERS LS&CO.	TOUCHTONE (DISNEY)	NUTRASWEET (G.D. SEARLE)

Case Study: Sony Brand Architecture

Sony chooses a single-minded, powerful, and yet flexible architecture and leverages their corporate brand in many different ways.

CORPORATE

SONY.

UMBRELLA AS DRIVER	ENDORSER BRAND	INGREDIENT BRAND	SHADOW ENDORSER	CO-BRAND

SONY PICTURES™

Sony Music

SONY
CLASSICAL ™

METREON®
A SONY ENTERTAINMENT CENTER

PRO
SONY

MEMORY STICK

Pro Audio

α

BRAVIA

Cyber-shot

PlayStation™

VAIO

XPERIA
Sony Smartphone

WALKMAN

Sony Ericsson

SONY BMG
MUSIC ENTERTAINMENT

07

10

41

22

142

06
Luxury Brand Marketing

What qualifies a brand as a luxury brand?

In economic terms, luxury products are those whose price/quality/service relationship is the highest on the markets or a product that can consistently command and justify a higher price than those with comparable functions and similar quality. There is always an argument for why some brands qualify as luxury and others are simply well known.

McKinsey defines luxury brands as those that "have constantly been able to justify a high price, i.e. significantly higher than the price of products with comparable tangible functions." This strict economic explanation does not help explain how well-known brands are differentiated from luxury brands. A Jaguar is considered less expensive than a Porsche, but in terms of comparable tangible functions it has a much stronger luxury brand image than Porsche. For some reason, Porsche is fast and expensive, just not luxury. A Breitling watch is generally more expensive than a watch from Tiffany, Hermès, or Gucci, yet it is often perceived as prestigious, not luxurious.

**THE HERMÈS BIRKIN HANDBAG
IS LUXURIOUS**

**THE COACH BAG
IS NOT**

Luxury used to belong to a few privileged few. Not any more. It's no longer about simply fashion goods, wine, jewelry, handbags, and accessories. Luxury is transforming scores of markets. It comes in many forms, at many price levels, and through a variety of channels, no longer confined to a few upscale shops on Rodeo Drive, Fifth Avenue, or Bond Street. Almost every marketer needs to consider whether or not they have a luxury brand strategy in place.

The question is:
Who will be the first one to effectively capture this segment in your category?

Luxury hasn't changed. What's changing is its definition. Once closely associated with high price, prestige, and ostentation, as large segments of consumers move upscale and luxury goods move downscale, we're seeing an explosive growth in what is being called the "massification of luxury goods."

The massification of luxury has been the single most important marketing phenomenon of modern times. It goes beyond what we see today: marketers connecting luxury to products that were never in that league. Advertising and packaging common products with words such as gourmet, premium, classic, gold, and platinum means that all consumers, whether they can afford true luxury or not, get a taste of the tantalizing. And thanks to eBay, more and more people have access to the finer, once out-of-reach things in life at an affordable price.

If anyone can afford it does it cease to be luxury? The answer is, definitely not. It only makes such items that much more desirable. Social philosophers like Pierre Bourdieu have shown the relationship between consumption, class, and identity. In creating one's identity and place in the world, few things in life proclaim status and superiority than purchasing, owning, and displaying luxury goods.

Old
Luxury

SLAVES TO
BRANDS

A VERY SMALL
SEGMENT

ONLY FOR THE
VERY RICH

SUPERB
CRAFTSMANSHIP,
HIGH QUALITY,
AND HIGH SERVICE

ONLY AVAILABLE
IN SELECT
UPSCALE SHOPS

New Luxury

WANTS QUALITY
AND SERVICE
AT ALL PRICE POINTS

BUYS THEM
THROUGH MULTIPLE
CHANNELS
AT MULTIPLE PRICE
POINTS

FIERCELY LOYAL,
ALWAYS LOOK
FOR A BRAND'S
HERITAGE

LESS ABOUT
CONSPICUOUS
CONSUMPTION AND
MORE ABOUT
SELF-RESPECT AND
FULFILLING
PERSONAL
EMOTIONAL NEEDS

Marketing is the ultimate social practice of postmodern consumer culture.
It plays a key role in giving meaning to life through consumption.

So is marketing too important to be left to marketers alone?

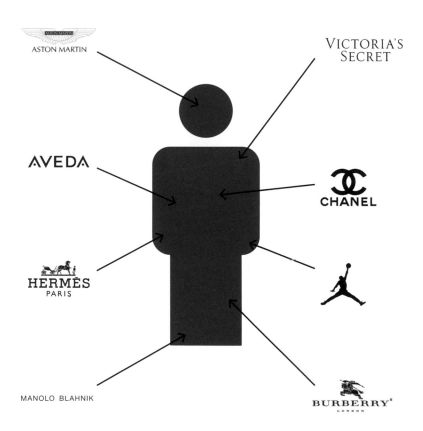

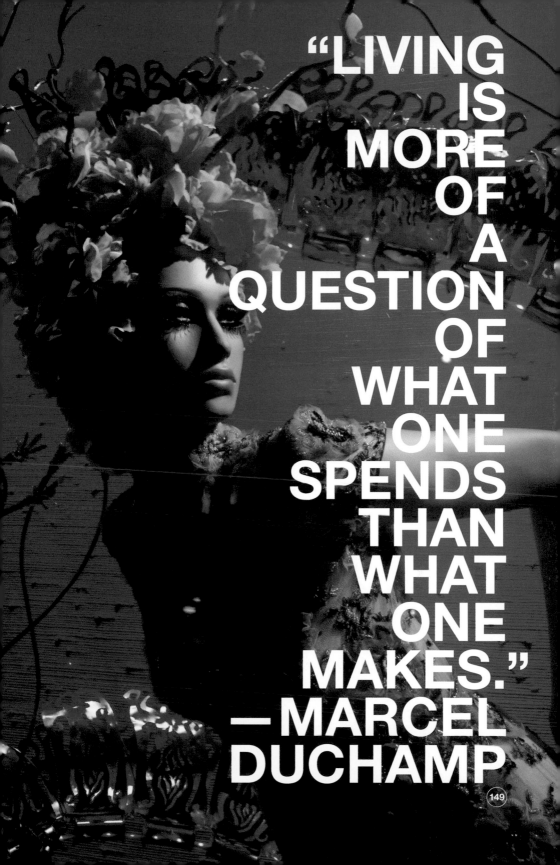

"LIVING IS MORE OF A QUESTION OF WHAT ONE SPENDS THAN WHAT ONE MAKES."
—MARCEL DUCHAMP

Fit in. Be Cool.

The standard of judgment becomes the ability to interact effectively with others, to win their affection and admiration—to merge with others of the same lifestyle.

What is important:
Can you consume the right brands?

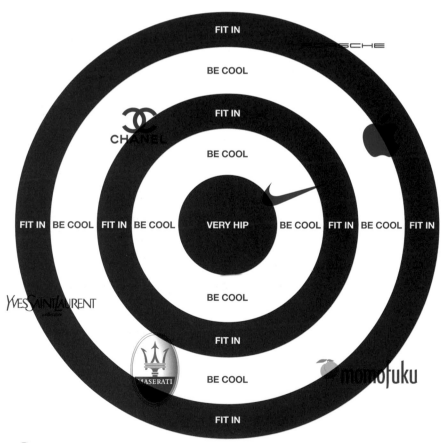

As a brand marketer, your job is to construct, maintain, and communicate identity and social meanings to others.

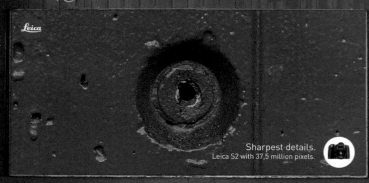

Sharpest details.
Leica S2 with 37,5 million pixels.

VALENTINO

Dior

Dior Addict

2

NIKE

AIR REINVENTED.
THE MOST FLEXIBLE
AIR MAX EVER.

AIR MAX+

153

In the old culture, the limited production capacity of the economy sharply reduced aspirations to material comfort. Today, much greater material satisfaction lies within the reach of even those of modest means.

Thus a *producer* culture becomes a *consumer* culture.

Product → Process

Problem Resolution → Emotion Seeking

AmericanGirl

Take home a
picture worth a
thousand smiles!

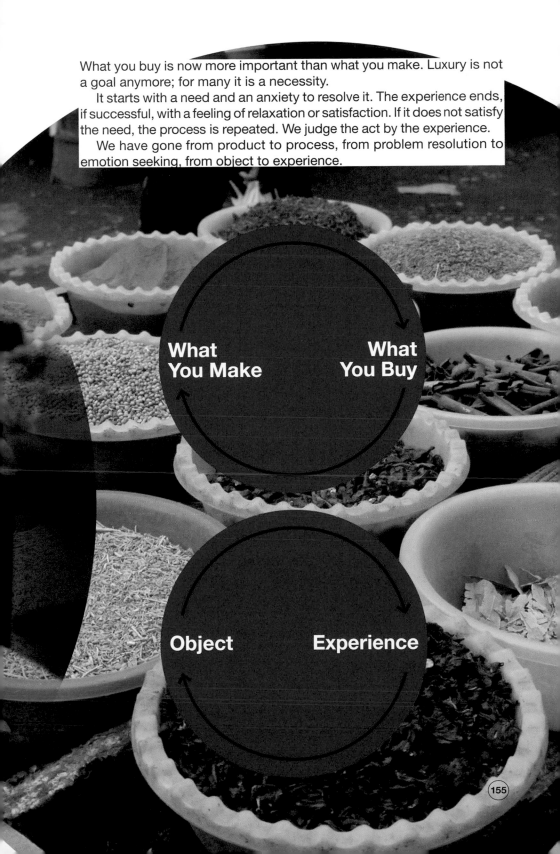

What you buy is now more important than what you make. Luxury is not a goal anymore; for many it is a necessity.

It starts with a need and an anxiety to resolve it. The experience ends, if successful, with a feeling of relaxation or satisfaction. If it does not satisfy the need, the process is repeated. We judge the act by the experience.

We have gone from product to process, from problem resolution to emotion seeking, from object to experience.

What You Make

What You Buy

Object

Experience

"Any kind of possession really functions, in a sense, as an extension of our personal power. It serves to make us feel stronger... When you watch a small child cling to a piece of cloth or a doll with all its power you may begin to understand the power of ownership."
—Ernest Dichter,
The Soul of Things

We Now Live in Consumption Communities

We are no longer divided by wealth, birth, or political eminence but by consumption. For marketers, brands and products need to be positioned to be bought, not made.

157

THE MASSIFICATION AND DEMOCRATIZATION OF LUXURY HAS BEEN THE SINGLE MOST IMPORTANT MARKETING PHENOMENON OF MODERN TIMES.

Consumption sometimes operates at a level of the imaginary, but it can also have "real" effects in facilitating the construction of self-identity.

Luxury shoppers are led by rational desires to purchase items of high value and craftsmanship. Eight of the ten top purchase motivators are emotionally driven. Marketers must tap into consumers' desires for well-being, self-concept, and indulgence. The consumption of symbolic meaning, reinforced through advertising, provides the individual with the opportunity to construct, maintain, and communicate identity and social meanings. Victoria's Secret is a great example of using the unobtainable, imaginary dreams of its consumers to drive sales. When beautiful and perfectly proportioned models strut down the runway and grace glossy catalog pages, they say that the company's products can enhance or even instill such glamour. If Victoria's Secret products are worn by the beautiful, does the inverse also hold true? Will wearing them make one beautiful?

Ask this important question: What are your key target segments' wildest imaginations?

8 of the top 10 purchase motivators are emotionally driven.

Just as a product fulfills its ability to satisfy a physical need, it must satisfy a symbolic need to create our meanings of our selves.

We become consumers of illusions.

De Beers' slogan, "A diamond is forever," has been so successful in creating the illusion of eternal love that a diamond is that illusion's material symbol. Now marketers are trying to do the same with platinum.

Ask this important question:
What illusions does your product help consumers to create or maintain?

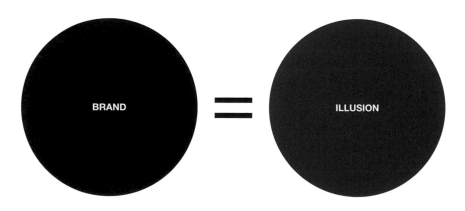

We become consumers of illusions

DE BEERS A DIAMOND IS FOREVER	=	♥
VICTORIA'S SECRET	=	XXX
Disney	=	🙂
Ferrari	=	24hrs
★ CONVERSE®	=	
CHANEL	=	\$\$\$
 ASTON MARTIN	=	

The symbolic meanings of products operate in two directions: outward in constructing the social world, and inward in constructing our self-identity.

Products help us become our possible selves.

Most SUVs and sports brand images are built on the very powerful concept of becoming ourselves, just better. SUVs speak to "sporty," "powerful," "tough," and "rugged." They appeal to men (and some women) who may not travel anywhere more treacherous than the local super-market. The Hummer sold to civilians is radically different from the one used by the military, yet the brand's image, as an enduring, robust all-terrain vehicle remains intact. Expensive and "cool," SUVs hold a carpool full of kids and their hockey equipment without saddling their upscale owners with a minivan.

Ask this important question: What are your target luxury segments' ideal possible selves?

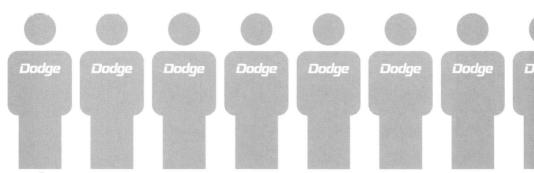

**PRODUCTS
HELP US
TO BECOME
OUR
POSSIBLE
SELVES.**

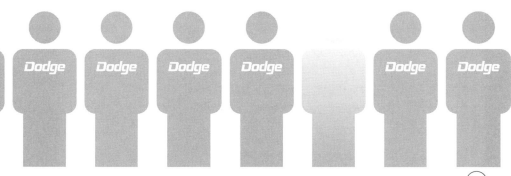

Advertising often provides gratification and recodes a commodity as a desirable psycho-ideological ideal. In fact, it feeds the desire to achieve the often unobtainable unity of the self, using destabilized meanings and images that separate products from their original intended use and offer the opportunity to reconstruct a self by purchasing meanings in a do-it-yourself fashion. Desire exists in the gap between visual languages and the unconscious.

Desire does not want satisfaction. To the contrary, desire desires desire. Images are often so appealing that things cannot satisfy. Some people desire desirelessness with such a passion that it actually increases their ability to desire. What we do we become stronger in, and these people yearn so much and so often to have no more yearning that their ability to yearn becomes astronomical. Postmodern consumption is inextricably linked with aspects of sexuality, both conscious and subconscious. Desires are constructed through linkages between consumption and the human body. Visuals continue to be the most powerful tool because they never satisfy. Calvin Klein, Gucci, and Abercrombie & Fitch built and maintain their brands based entirely on this concept. Meaning is created through a continuous search for links between identity (social) and the self.

Ask this important question:
What are the unobtainable desires that your brands are based on?

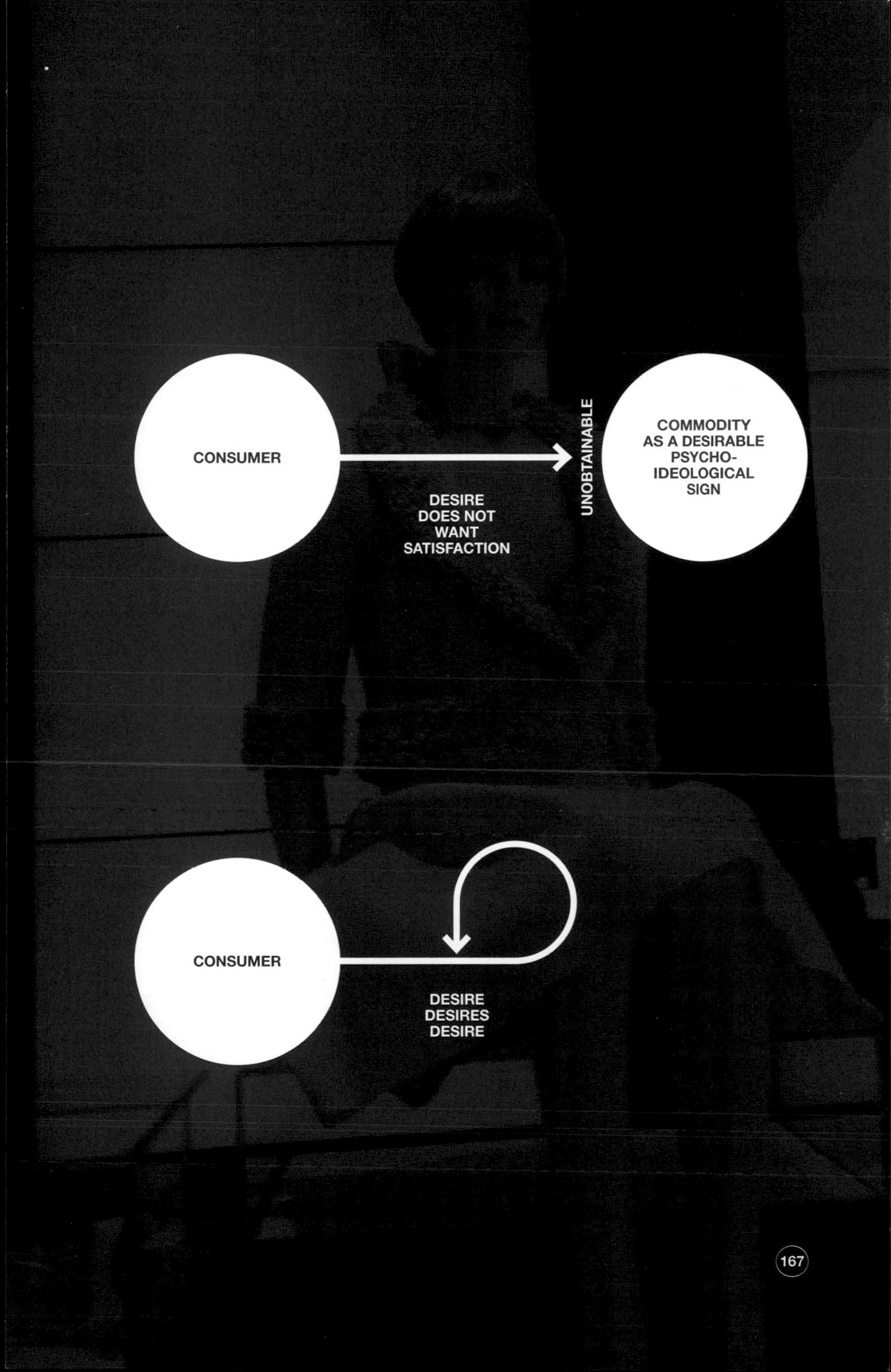

CONSUMER

DESIRE
DOES NOT
WANT
SATISFACTION

UNOBTAINABLE

COMMODITY
AS A DESIRABLE
PSYCHO-
IDEOLOGICAL
SIGN

CONSUMER

DESIRE
DESIRES
DESIRE

The expansion of "wants" reduces our choice to "want not" and sometimes makes the very idea of rational choice meaningless. We're in the era of the "empty-self," in which alienation can be solved by the "lifestyle" solution, in which we construct a "self" by purchasing even limited rationality.

Calvin Klein Jeans

Materialism versus Spiritualism

We use all kinds of tools everyday. We are tool users and tools are not the end but the means. So materialism does not crowd out spiritualism; spiritualism is more likely a substitute when objects are scarce. When we have fewer things, we make the next world luxurious. When we have plenty, we enchant those objects around us.

exclusively in Louis Vuitton stores and on louisvuitton.com. 866-VUITTON

LOUIS VUITTON

If this is the case, then the current weak version of experience co-creation (which is still more like mass configuration at this point, despite its own protestations to the contrary) may give way to what I have been calling "deep co-creation," in which customers not only co-create the experience and some of the value, but the business itself (and, by extension the brand). And they will of course do this as a large, interconnected community. So in this changed world, a big part of people's meaning might come from co-creating a business and seeing it thrive.
—Christian Briggs

"Luxury comes from exclusivity. Individualism equals exclusivity. So by definition, every time a brand gives room to consumers to express their individualism, it becomes an exclusive, luxurious good. This will lead to a future of consumers using their self-expression to get the luxury into pretty much any brand in their brandsphere."
—Bart Suichies

"'What constitutes luxury becomes a wholly individual and emotional decision.' Clearly the rules of luxury are not set exclusively by a few educated minds anymore. Experience is luxury. Silence is luxury. To some, not mentioning the word luxury is luxury. Very human. Not so engineer-friendly."
—Flavio Azeved

21

55

06

49

Strategic Branding Process

30

Developing a Brand Strategy

Building a distinctive and high-performing brand has never been as difficult or resource-consuming as it is today. With the proliferation of technology and social media, the bar continues to rise, and customers are now exposed to ever increasing numbers and varieties of messages. In today's environment, brand strategy can no longer be created and managed solely by marketing and brand managers. Go-it-alone brand efforts will likely fail. The whole organization must collaborate from strategy development to execution. This book provides a process for a cross-functional planning effort.

We must take a fundamentally new approach to brand building in order to close the gap. An integrated cross-functional approach to brand strategy development that fuses deep customer insights and segmentation, evolving business economics, and customer experience design capability is required. Companies must direct their resources to these efforts to win in these hyper-competitive markets.

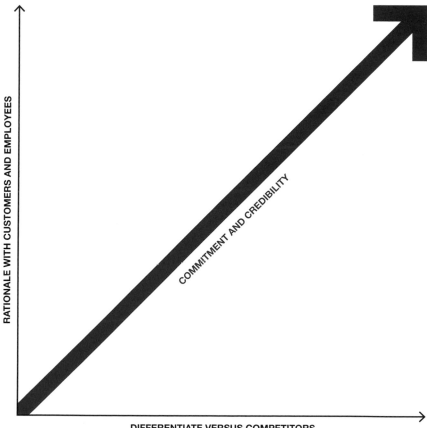

Branding Is a Business Process

Branding is a business process—one that is planned, strategically focused, and integrated throughout the organization. Branding establishes the direction, leadership, clarity of purpose, inspiration, and energy for a company's most important asset—its brand. Even the most powerful strategy will fail if not communicated effectively and consistently. Ultimately, how the brand is interpreted and expressed is in customer experience design, and all forms of communication will bring it to life. Whether communications are formal or informal, the objective is to speak with one consistent voice that embraces the brand's essence, which can be manifested in the customer experience. To maximize its effectiveness, your brand must be understood by key audiences: customers, prospects, business partners, regulators, analysts, the media, employees, and all other groups that determine the viability of your company to do business and can be translated into action both externally and internally.

Everyone in the company must live up to the brand promise. This concept is simple but it is all-encompassing—it's about every company member being a walking, talking reflection of the brand itself. When clearly articulated, a brand's position becomes a rallying cry for employees and helps them during times of challenge and change. This moves you one step closer to a brand-driven organization. Organizations that succeed in building a brand-driven culture usually have strong motivation and reward systems in place to keep managers and front line people interested in exploring better brand decisions.

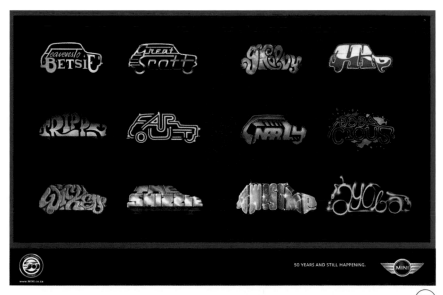

Before You Start!
A brand strategy is not the consequence of planning, but the opposite: it's the starting point. Here are the three basic requirements:

Requirement One
A clearly articulated business strategy with a view of the scale and scope of the business and how you want to compete.

Requirement Two
Deep customer insights and understanding of evolving business economics. This requires you to look at the evolving nature of different target segments and their existing and potential profitability.

Requirement Three
Determine the role of branding as perceived by your corporation to help shape many strategic brand decisions during the development process.

Step 01
Extract Explicit Short- and Long-Term Business Goals as Drivers of Brand Vision

Step 02
Conduct Key Stakeholder Analysis to Capture Implicit Brand Requirements

Step 03
Develop Customer Needs– Driven Segmentation with Perspectives on Competition and Segment Economics

Step 04
Develop a Brand Vision Linked to the Corporate or Business Unit Business Strategy

Step 05
Develop a Brand Promise

Step 06
Develop Brand Positioning

Step 07
Develop Brand Personality

Step 08
Develop Brand Narrative

Step 09
Develop a Brand Identity System

Step 10
Translate Brand Promise into Customer Experience Design

	Internal	**External**
Fixed	Brand Vision **What do we want our brand to become?**	Brand Promise **What is our commitment to our customers, our employees, and the world?**
Variable	Brand Delivery **How do we intend to fulfill our commitment and what actions will we take?**	Brand Positioning **How do we want to be perceived and what are our competitive advantages?**

Step 01
Extract Explicit Short- and Long-Term Business Goals as Drivers of Brand Vision

A common pitfall is not to have a long-term business strategy. At the very least, you should have an articulated description of the business and know how it creates value and competes in its chosen industries. An effective strategy acts as a bridge between the past and the future. It involves judgments and decisions about when to commit and bet, when to delay a commitment, when to abort a plan that won't work, and when to change the rules of the game. Strategy is a complex system of acting and talking, a system that occasionally manifests itself in rational designs. Many brand strategy development efforts are unintentionally turned into corporate strategy discussions. As a result these efforts are blamed for not delivering any value. WARNING! You cannot develop a meaningful brand strategy in the absence of a business strategy. You can create a name, a logo, tag lines, and a set of graphic elements for brand identification purposes to deal with short-term marketing communications needs, but you need a brand strategy for the long term.

Step 02
Conduct Key Stakeholder Analysis to Capture Implicit Brand Requirements

Stakeholder management is an important discipline that successful managers use to win support from others. A branding project is no different. Stakeholder analysis is the technique used to identify the key people who have to be won over. The first step is to identify who your key stakeholders are. It might include the CEO, CMO, CFO, VP Brand, VP Marketing, VP Customer Experience, and VP Operations.

The next step is to work out stakeholder power, influence, interest, and intent. The final step is to develop a good understanding of the most important stakeholders so you know their requirements, and can win their support. Record this analysis on a stakeholder map.

The benefits of using a stakeholder-based approach is that you can use the opinions of the most powerful stakeholders to shape your branding projects at an early stage. Not only does this make it more likely that they will support you, their input also improves the quality of your project and helps you to gain the resources needed. By communicating with them early and frequently you ensure that they fully understand what you are doing and the related benefits.

Step 03
Develop Customer Needs–Driven Segmentation with Perspectives on Competition and Segment Economics

Most companies have developed customer segments either by needs, usage, or affordability. Often the results are not particularly useful because they are not economically viable or actionable. Segmentation must be based on the existing or potential profitability of the targeted segments. Companies should segment customers with the in-depth perspective of future economics of their industry. This may include segment growth, behavior, price, and service requirements. Any time a company tries to look at future economics, there is uncertainty about assumptions. A scenario-based planning approach is likely to create a better picture to support decision making. This provides direction as to where the company can take its brand in the future.

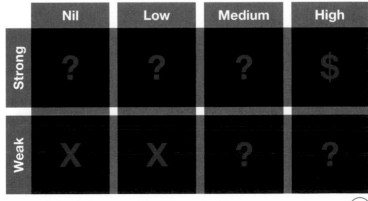

Step 04
Develop a Brand Vision Linked to the Corporate or Business Unit Business Strategy

Crafting a brand vision forces you to think through where you want the brand to be over the longer term to support your corporate strategy. It helps the management team achieve consensus on longer-term goals and the level of branding support that is required to achieve them. It also provides guidelines to determine what kind of research to put in place to monitor brand-building progress and return on investment. Most of all it gives you a starting point and a mandate to start developing other elements to support the delivery of the brand promise.

A brand vision statement has no fixed length or style of composition. It is relevant, and therefore specific to the business and the world within which it operates. A brand vision statement is by definition long-term and transcends particular products, markets, or even current executive leadership. A brand vision statement should be complementary to the company's vision statement; sometimes the two are combined. Ultimately, it is the interconnection between aspirations, values, and the brand that is important, not what the statement is called. It must be simple enough that your customers understand it, and your people get it—and remember it.

CISCO

The most trusted technology company in the world, Cisco is a leader in delivering personal and business video that transforms life's experiences.

At IKEA our vision is to create a better everyday life for the [sic] many people. Our business idea supports this vision by offering a wide range of well-designed, functional home furnishing products at prices so low that as many people as possible will be able to afford them.

"Inventing the future of play"'

We want to pioneer new ways of playing,
play materials, and the business models of play
leveraging globalisation and digitalisation ...
it is not just about products, it is about realising
the human possibility.

At IBM, we strive to lead in the creation, development, and manufacturing of the industry's most advanced information technologies, including computer systems, software, networking systems, storage devices, and microelectronics. We translate these advanced technologies into value for our customers through professional solutions and services businesses through the world.

SONY®

We Help Dreamers Dream

Sony is a company devoted to the CELEBRATION of life. We create things for every kind of IMAGINATION. Products that stimulate the SENSES and refresh the spirit. Ideas that always surprise and never disappoint. INNOVATIONS that are easy to love, and EFFORTLESS to use, things that are not essential, yet hard to live without. We are not here to be logical. Or predictable. We're here to pursue INFINITE possibilities. We allow the BRIGHTEST minds to interact freely, so the UNEXPECTED can emerge. We invite new THINKING so even more fantastic ideas can evolve. CREATIVITY is our essence. We take chances. We EXCEED expectations. We help dreamers DREAM.

Step 05
Develop a Brand Promise

The basis of any brand is its core promise, the essential idea around which the components of the brand are built. It is a promise to achieve certain results, deliver a certain experience, or act in a certain way. The brand promise has to be something that is relevant to your paying customers and they actually care about. It should be clear with no room for misinterpretation, and customers and employees hearing or reading it will "get" it without explanation. This includes the frontline employee who may know little about the brand, to the organization's senior management. It needs to be concise in language so everyone can remember it.

But notice something: the word *promise* is a lot more powerful than the word *strategy* or *performance*. That's because strategy and performance are about corporations. Promises are about people. A promise is conveyed by everything people see, hear, touch, taste, or smell about your business. Industries and competition evolve, but a brand lives on. Your company's greatest legacy is its brand. A brand promise is vital to articulating a higher calling, a crystal-clear positioning, a magnetic personality and an aspirational brand affiliation. These are the rational and emotional components of a powerful brand promise. The brand promise humanizes the mission statement and makes it easy for everyone in the organization to understand how the company creates value and how they impact the customer experience directly and indirectly in a way that adds or detracts value from it.

J. Walker Smith, executive chairman of The Futures Company and a leading consumer trends analyst, identified key trends in the consumer marketplace. Each statement refers to brands or brand promises directly or indirectly. Resist the easy temptation to over-extend a brand or use it where it can't keep its value promise. Once a brand's promise is broken, the trust relationship with its customers is damaged, perhaps permanently. Understand the promise a brand makes, and then pay fanatical attention to keeping that promise.

Old Icons consumers look for the familiar and comfortable

Plain Talk consumers want proof, not potential

Solidarity relevant themes are strength, resolve, fairness, and justice.

Politeness and courtesy matter

Feel-Good consumers want a connection beyond owning and having

Home Cockpits family and community take center stage

Consumables make it experiential or "more than more stuff." "Woo" rather than "wow"

Cloaking people are looking for private satisfaction or inconspicuous consumption

ıı|ıı.ı|ı.
CISCO

When customers think of Cisco, they think
of a company that brings people together
by removing the barriers to communication.
By connecting people Cisco can transform
our lives, making us more productive, engaged,
and powerful.

Everyone at HP is united by a single promise
we make to every customer—regardless of
who they are, where they are, or what they want
to achieve: We can help you do that.

What our brand promise means:

— We build true partnerships with customers,
and our work always begins with their goals
and challenges.

— We are straightforward in all that we do,
because we respect people and deliver clear
value to them.

— We believe in our customers' aspirations,
and we're confident in our ability to help make
them real.

pepsi®

Pepsi captures the excitement of now,
creating culture and embracing individuality.
Pepsi is being open to possibilities, trying
new things, and making the most of the moment.

NOKIA
Connecting People

Nokia, the trusted brand, creates personalized communication technology that enables people to shape their own mobile world. We also see mobile technology as an enabler to help create a more environmentally sound world.

The rise of mobile communications, combined with better product design, tighter control of production processes, and greater reuse of materials and recycling are all helping to reduce the use of scarce natural resources.

Many activities that currently use large amounts of energy and raw materials could be moved into the digital space to greatly reduce their environmental impact. Such new opportunities, however, come hand in hand with responsibility.

The core promise of the GE brand is "better living." Through its global, human, technical, and financial resources, GE applies the power of the mind and its creative capabilities to provide products and solutions that make life better.

GE has consistently made this promise to its customers for nearly a century. Throughout history, GE's marketing communications in both the consumer and commercial arenas have emphasized how GE's products make life better. In each case, the point is not the products but the core promise of better living.

GE communications are: Not about aircraft engines, but about the way that they bring together people of all nationalities and walks of life. Not about imaging equipment, but about how this equipment improves people's well being. Not about appliances, but about the convenience they provide and make life more enjoyable.

Overall, GE's core promise has been communicated with remarkable consistency and discipline for over a century. As a result, this core promise holds considerable equity, an equity that offers immense potential for global extensions.

Step 06
Develop Brand Positioning

Look at the meaning of your brand. Look at how it is perceived in the minds of consumers relative to competition and the perceptual difference between customer segments and product categories. Explore the extent to which your brand's perception is favorable to your present and future customer segments as well as its consistency within product categories —up and down the value chain. This analytical process is based on the following four key questions:

What is the brand for?
The meaning of your brand.

Who is the brand for?
Your most profitable segments.

When is the brand for?
The occasion when the purchase or consumption takes place.

Who are the brand's competitors?
Who are the direct and indirect competitors
that threaten your brand's mind, heart, and market share?

Once you develop a full understanding of what's in your customers' minds, it is easy to examine what has worked in the past and then evaluate the effectiveness of efforts to differentiate your brand and position it to target desirable customer segments.

Two of the key drivers to building brand strength are creating a distinct brand identity and developing a unique brand personality with their associated images. Unfortunately, semantics often impedes understanding of how these two factors influence brand strategy. Brand identity, for example, is often used in a limited, graphic-centric manner or is used interchangeably with brand image. Identity is often seen as just the graphics, logos, colors, and symbols that make up corporate identity. Those elements are the appearance (which is very important) but not the substance of a brand, just as the clothes you wear are an important, even distinguishing, part of your identity, but not the substance of who you are as a person.

Step 06

An obsession with image tends to attach greater importance to appearance than to inner reality. But brand identity is a richer, more substantive concept. The two concepts are quite different. There's also a simple way to sum up and understand the essence of the two terms: image is how the marketplace perceives you; identity is who you really are. Companies are advised to focus on building brand identity as the driving brand-strategy component. Brand image is not diminished at all. It is, after all, how a company is perceived. But don't make the mistake of thinking your brand image is your identity. The challenge for brand strategists and champions is to align image and identity. That happens—and can only happen—through careful, proactive management of your brand identity components.

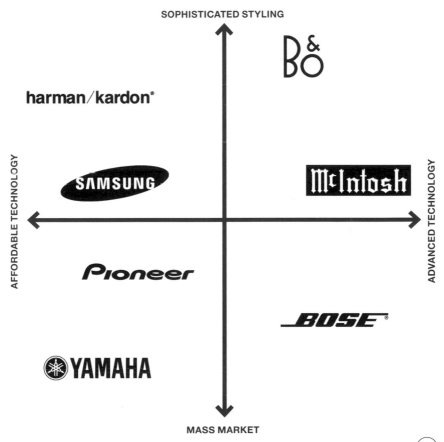

Step 06

Mountain Dew Positioning Statement

To <u>young, active soft-drink consumers</u> (Relevant Market Segments) who have little time for sleep, <u>Mountain Dew</u> (Brand) is the <u>soft drink</u> (Frame of Reference) that gives you <u>more energy</u> (Competitive Edge) than any other brand because it has the highest level of caffeine. With Mountain Dew, you can <u>stay alert</u> (Competitive Edge) and keep going even when you haven't been able to get a good night's sleep.

Step 06

Dove
Positioning Statement

Beauty. It's not about <u>glamour or fame</u> (Points of Differentiation). It's about every <u>woman</u> (Relevant Market Segments) and the <u>beauty</u> (Frame of Reference) that is in each of us. That's what <u>Dove</u> (Brand) is all about. And that's why more women <u>trust</u> (Competitive Edge) their skin to Dove.

Step 07
Develop Brand
Personality

Brand personality is the way a brand expresses, interacts, and behaves with certain human personality traits. It's when the brand image or brand identity is expressed in terms of human traits. Virgin is adventurous, fun, and irreverent; Dove is honest, feminist, and optimist; and Hewlett-Packard represents accomplishment, reliability, and straightforwardness. Brand personality is that aspect of comprehensive brand that generates its emotional character and associations in consumer minds. It creates engagement by establishing a shared aspiration or value between your audience and your brand. It is reflected from the totality of consumer experiences with the brand. It is unique and remembered for a long time. Once you have identified your brand's personality as it currently is, you can explore ways to develop the tone of voice that is an appropriate extension of your brand and will reach your audience on a human level, encouraging positive dialogue and injecting empathy into the brand.

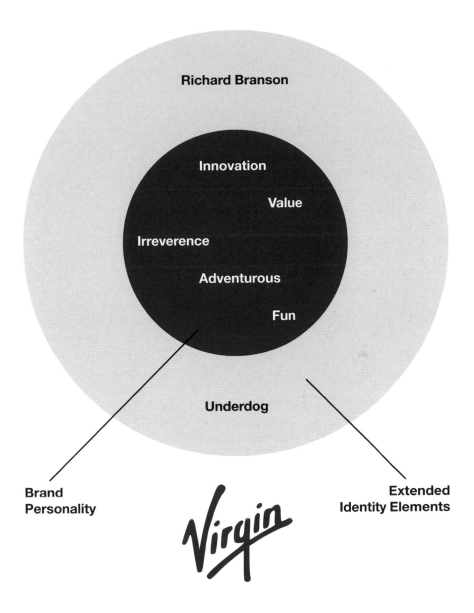

Virgin stands for irreverence, individuality, freedom loving, and anti-establishment. Consequently the company seeks out all markets in which these values are important: as a global brand, Virgin possesses a strong brand identity that cannot easily be copied. Virgin targets markets that are controlled cartels and that operate under the pseudo-competitive environment of a duopoly. They see potential profits to be made in these markets by a new player who does not play by the rules.

Step 08
Develop Brand Narrative

Brand narratives are not usually a formal part of a brand strategy and are often used by marketers unconsciously. People are exposed to brand narratives daily; it is the story of the ideas, experiences, and values that represent the tangible, authentic depth, emotional connections, and integrity of the brand's relationship with its consumers, staff, and other stakeholders. It is part of the process of brand storytelling and can be used by senior executives or brand managers to guide strategy and creative development, or in marketing and communications to bring meaning and authenticity to a campaign. The brand narrative is a co-creation, started by the company but ultimately joined and improvised by the consumers and the brand communities.

Your brand narrative is what people say about you, and how they connect emotionally with your product or service. Social media platforms provide a nearly perfect arena for this sort of interactive storytelling. These platforms allow people to connect with products that reinforce their values or identity. The old school of marketing uses the oversimplified approach that a brand should own a "word." The idea is that a brand can only stand for one thing in the mind of the market. This is irrelevant in today's world, as it is becoming impossible for a brand to own a "word." Volvo used to own the word "Safety" and they are also into sports. Porsche used to own the word "Sports" and they are also into family cars. Identifying one simplistic position and communicating it in a repetitive manner is an outdated approach. Positioning can be used to identify a positioning in the marketplace, but it should not be the single guiding factor.

When the CMO of McDonald's, Larry Light, talked about the new branding strategy behind McDonald's incredible turn-around story, he described McDonald's' new marketing approach as "Brand Journalism."

The brand narrative is the most relevant expression of the brand and forms the core for trans-media collective storytelling that delivers brand-centric, customer-relevant, humanized, interesting, accessible content in any format and at any time that your audience wants to consume it that builds a brand.

Step 09
Develop a Brand
Identity System

Brand identity encompasses all the visual aspects that form the overall brand and its expressions. Brand identity stems from the organization; it is responsible for creating a distinguished product with unique characteristics. It is how an organization seeks to identify itself and a graphic manifestation of its brand strategy and personality. It consists of a logo that identifies a business or product system in its simplest form via the use of a mark or icon and extends into uniform interior and interfaces. In most cases, identity design is based around the visual devices used within a company, usually assembled within a set of graphic guidelines, including the use of photography and tone of writing. These guidelines that make up an identity usually administer how the identity is applied throughout different mediums, limiting to an approved color palette system, fonts, layouts, use of space, and so forth. These guidelines ensure that the identity of the company is kept coherent, which in turn allows the brand as a whole to be recognizable.

Logo

The Cisco logo should work across all media. The style you choose will depend on the environment in which the logo appears. To ensure the expression of the logo is right for its context, we've created a system that includes PANTONE® color, and an extended palette of solid colors as well as gradients as well as reversed logo treatments. So whether the Cisco logo appears on packaging, the Web, TV, in print, on screen, or on a product, you have near infinite design flexibility to adapt the logo to its appropriate design context.

EXTENDED LOGO PALETTE
The palettes to the right provide an example of how color can be infused into the logo. These are only partial palettes. For complete palettes, please refer to the following Color section.

PMS 7477 + PMS 7477	PMS 7477	BLACK	REVERSED

PREFERRED PALETTE / SOLID

PREFERRED PALETTE / GRADIENTS

Logo

Clear Space

Maximum Size

Minimum Size

Give it space. To preserve the integrity and visual impact of the Cisco logo, always maintain adequate clear space around it. The clear space around the logo is an integral part of its design, and ensures the logo can be seen quickly, uncluttered by other logos, symbols, artwork, or text.

Too big, too much. When using the Cisco logo in large-scale formats, it is important only to include the trademark ™ symbol up to 3-3/4". Anything larger and the trademark symbol will begin to compete against the mark itself.

Too small, not enough. To ensure that the Cisco logo and its trademark symbol reproduce legibly at smaller scales, only include the trademark ™ symbol down to 3/4". The trademark symbol will not reproduce legibly at any size smaller than 3/4". For all print and on-screen applications, remove the trademark symbol completely.

Step 10
Translate Brand Promise into Customer Experience Design

Companies invest considerable time, money, and energy into developing a brand promise that differentiates them from the competition. Yet, if employees can't translate the results into their customer interactions or experiences, this exercise is futile. How can companies expect their frontline employees to be brand ambassadors unless they understand what the promise is and how to deliver it? It also needs to be reflected in customer interfaces as well as physical space design. Additionally, you need to be honest about where the organization stands. Do not make the mistake of developing a grandiose brand promise that you cannot keep.

Although you must combine vision with reality, you should not take weakness in any particular dimension as an excuse to do nothing. No company gets it right all the time. Indeed, the best brand leaders consider recovery from service failures a critical element of the experience they deliver. You cannot translate your brand promise into a working service blueprint without working in cross-functional teams and including people in the field. This gives them a sense of ownership and raises their level of commitment. Customer experience design is not a one-off exercise; it is ongoing and needs to be supported by the right organizational culture and structure.

commenting stations

tasting

lecter and commenting bar

2

bench

bench

bench

40

23

33

52

08
Strategic Branding Assessment

This quick approach to brand assessment is a self-diagnostic tool to allow you to make a quick assessment of the strength of your brands. The scoring and findings of this quick assessment will provide a better understanding of overall brand strength and will allow you to devise more effective brand-building strategies and programs. This is clearly not meant as a means to evaluate product functions or features. It is meant solely to focus on the issues that influence the intangible values of your products, customers, and markets— the issues that generally have an influence on, and are embedded in, brands. In conducting this examination, think about where your brand stands today. For a department- or company-wide assessment, add up the total scores and divide them by the number of respondents. I suggest that you separate departmental responses to gain a better picture of the gaps between departments or business units. A scoring guide is at the end of the questionnaire.

01 Clear statement of complete brand purpose and direction:
Yes   0
Not yet   2

02 Brand personality and values known and understood:
Yes   0
More intuitive   1
Not really   2

03 Top management outside brand and marketing functions supports the brand-building efforts:
Strong   0
Adequate   2
Pretty shaky   4

04 Internal brand champion:
Strong champion with authority   0
A champion with responsibility   1
Unofficial champion   2
Simply does not exist   3

05 Internal planning policies and procedures:
Strategic and disciplined   0
Pretty strong overall   1
Need certain improvements   2
Basically ad hoc and tactical   3

06 Would you describe your company as:
Customer-driven   0
Brand-driven   0
Technology-driven   1
Sales-driven   2
Competitor-driven   3

07 Does your company consider brand building as:
A core business function   0
Synonymous with marketing   1
Marcom responsibility   3
A cost   4

08 Integration of marketing communications plans:
Planning done jointly   0
Coordinated, not well integrated   1
Not done; needs improvement   3

09 Long-term brand vision:
Clear and emotive	0
Vision exists but always referred to	2
Identity guidelines exist	4

10 Explicit brand promise:
Well defined and crafted	0
Well defined/needs support	1
Exists but not too credible	2
Does not exist	3

11 Emotive brand story:
Brand story is known and authentic	0
Good story but less authenticity	1
A product story more than a brand story	2
Nonexistent	4

12 Product/brand segmentation strategy:
Very clear and well defined	0
Yes, but not effectively	1
Overly fragmented, too many	2
Does not exist at all	3

13 Marketing support and communications budget:
Enough to do the job	0
Insufficient to achieve our goal	1
It comes and goes	2
Severely under-resourced	4

14 Brand marketing investment ROI:
Have a very good idea	0
Limited to soft measurement	1
Periodically measure results	2
Absolutely no idea	3

15 All marketing communications are integrated:
Overall well integrated	0
Needs more improvement	1
Depends on vendors and timing	2
Integration is not possible at all	3

16 Knowledge of customer:
Good feedback system in place	0
Adequate research done	1
We should be doing more	3

17 Committed, profitable customers:
Strong loyalty, measured   0
Competitive enough   1
Who really knows?   3

18 Brand awareness:
High awareness in key markets   0
Okay, but could be better   1
Not at competitive levels   3

19 Brand quality perceptions:
Clearly the brand quality leader   0
Perceived as quality brand   1
Not one of our strengths   4

20 Familiarity:
Most of our target knows us well   0
It's getting better   1
Way below what it should be   3

21 Internal understanding of what our brand stands for:
Most staff have a good idea   0
Only the marketing folks know   1
Nobody has any idea   3

22 Brand image and personality:
Have a desirable image   0
Image could be in tighter focus   1
Not clear or well defined   3

23 Associations attached to the brand:
Strong associations   0
Differentiated but not strong   1
Undifferentiated and weak   3

24 Overall customer experiences are aligned with the brand:
Customer experience reflects the brand   0
Sometimes but not consistent   1
Very disconnected   3

25 Does the brand reflect organizational culture:
Brand values reflect culture   0
To some extent but not sure   1
Not at all   3

Add up your score for each question. If multiple people are taking the assessment, tally the scores and use the average to determine where your brand or brands fall in the "strength range." Do not mix the scores of different functional departments. Comparison can be drawn between functions as well as between senior management and the marketing department. Be aware, however, that it's not really the score that's most helpful here; it is a matter of looking at the individual responses to each question, determining the most pressing issues and prioritizing actions to take. True performance comes from a focus on the brand-influencing activities and actions that are strengthened through consistent and conscientious work on an ongoing basis.

0–19 Points
Robust, strong, and most likely enjoying brand leadership

20–34 Points
Commendable perfor-mance—but could use more focused work

35–49 Points
Just getting by, too weak—needs help from outside

50+ Points
Faint, weak brand—brand overhaul and a brand-driven cultural transformation are needed

12

35

05

46

09

Strategic
Brand Audit

27

Brand Name	
Brand Auditor	
Brand Owner	
Audit Date	
Audit Period	

53

What Is a Brand Audit?

A brand audit provides a systematic way of understanding what brands are and what added values they offer, both to the consumer and the company. The following is a simple and highly effective approach that can be used to evaluate the business performance of your brand. The brand audit has three components. The first is the brand inventory, which is a brand-specific situation analysis and a description of all the marketing input. The second is brand exploration, which is a detailed description of the consumer perception of the brand. The third part is analysis. The analysis is a reaction to the first two parts, essentially what can be learned by comparing what management has planned, hoped, and done with what consumers feel, believe, and do. The specifics of a brand audit vary; here a general approach is provided, which can be used to guide you through a do-it-yourself brand audit.

Marketing managers started doing audits of marketing plans and market conditions soon after the modern-day disciplines were established in the 1950s and 1960s. As the approach to brand strategy and management has evolved, these audits have focused on more detailed measures of brand and category value, sustainability, and brand position risk.

223

While the importance of brand asset value and brand equity is widely accepted, the practical measures and operating issues that drive these end results are not always well developed. Here we've used five measures as scorecard foundations for brand and category management; other measures can be built on these:

01 Category Relevance
Brands have meaning and value with customers in the context of a market category.

02 Competitive Differentiation
The brand's combined sense of advantage and value proposition that is relevant to the core target customers.

03 Investment in Brand Assets
The nature of investments in product and customer experience that adds to brand equity.

04 Integration of Positioning
Making clear the nature of the brand's purpose and the assured customer experience.

05 Prospects for Brand Evolution
The natural transformation of brands over time in different market conditions and degrees of globalization.

What are the objectives for the brand and how has brand management performed to achieve these objectives?

Situation Issues

What is the single most important challenge for the brand? Identify the competitive brands. Describe and forecast their brand marketing strategies.

How have the competitive brands evolved over time?

What is the nature and basis of brand customer relationships if they do exist?

Who are the customers? How have customer perceptions changed over time and what shaped them? Identify any relevant drivers for suppliers, buyers, customers, technology, regulations, or other environmental factors that might be relevant to the brand.

Product Issues

What products bear the brand name?

What is the nature and what are the qualities of these products?

What are the key attributes of the branded products?

What is the brand structure? (Family, corporate, umbrella, etc.)

What is the intended positioning of the branded products relative to their competitors?

What does the price signal about the brand?

What do the distribution outlets signal about the brand?

Customer Experience and Communications Issues

How has the customer experience matched the customer perceptions or expectations?

_____

How has the brand manifested itself in the digital world?

_____

How has the interface reflected our brand personality?

_____

How consistent are customer communications across all channels?

_____

How has the brand message been communicated?

_____

What are the prominent brand themes in communication?

_____

What are the qualities of the media and media vehicles?

_____

Describe the management of brand elements—symbols, logos, packages, product design, style.

_____

Sources:
— Interviews with company personnel.
— Interviews with channel partners.
— Company documents.
— Business publications, trade journals.
— Expert opinions.
— Tangible marketing: products, ads, observations of distribution, promotions, and your expert analysis of them.

02 Brand Exploration

What is the overall likeability of the brand?

___

What is the overall brand awareness level?

___

What is consumer response to the brand?

___

What is the channel partner response to the brand?

___

What do they believe about the brand's claims —
its attributes and benefits?

___

What other associations do people have to the brand?

___

How much do consumers value brand equity?

___

What are consumer motives toward or away from the brand?

___

Consider the competition; what do consumers view
as substitutes? Conduct a consumer perceptions analysis,
identifying the strengths and weaknesses of the brand.

___

Describe consumer behavior with respect to brand–market
share, places where the brand is bought, relevant information
sources, and uses for the brand.

___

What is the perceived brand identity?

___

What is the perceived brand image/personality?

___

What is the image of users of the brand?

___

What is the image of the company behind the brand for customers?

___

What is the image of the company behind the brand from
the perspectives of the employees?

___

There are two source types—baseline, or secondary, research sources and primary research sources. The former should provide general answers; the latter should be designed to address specific questions that you (a) think are important and (b) do not already have good answers for.

— **Research reports or summaries of past research provided by the company.**

— **Business publications, trade journals.**

— **Expert opinions and your own expert analysis.**

— **Primary data collection possibilities:**

    — **Awareness (decide on the appropriate measures.)**

    — **Brand associations**

    — **Image analysis/attitudes**

    — **Brand purchase motives (various indirect techniques; select appropriately)**

    — **Brand personality (both indirect and direct measures available)**

    — **Brand equity measures (again, several measures available; select appropriately)**

*Choice of primary data collection: The brand exploration should cover everything that is part of consumer brand knowledge, but it must definitively address all the aspects identified in the brand inventory. For example, if the brand inventory suggests a certain positioning strategy or assumes a specific purchase frequency, assess consumers' perceived positions or consumers' purchase frequency. Or, if you identify an opportunity that is not addressed in the brand inventory (e.g., an untapped segment), assess that possibility.

*Design of primary data collection: Your guideline is to conduct the research in the same way as the firm. A couple of aspects are flexible. One is sample size. Aim for a sample of 50, which is far less than practical but probably large enough to yield meaningful results. The other is data analysis. There is no need for fancy statistical tests. Frequencies and comparisons of scale means should cover everything. Make judgments about differences on the basis of practical, not statistical, effect sizes. Note, that you should make an effort to use an appropriate sample. Asking your fellow colleagues or your neighbors questions may be just fine for Harvey's or Hershey, but probably not for Hermès.

Are brand management elements consistent?

Do consumers have a clear and consistent image of the brand?

Do employees understand what the brand means and how
it is connected to how they do the job on a day-to-day basis?

Is the brand being over-extended to different products and
is being diluted?

Are we doing enough brand-building effort to ensure we are
still building brand equity?

Are there any changes in leadership, management structures, or
organizational design that are changing how the brand behaves?

Are consumers responding as management expected/hoped?
Identify and discuss the important successes and failures.

Make suggestions for changes in brand management, opportunities,
or threats in the marketplace that need to be addressed,
opportunities for developing or extending brand equity, and
possibilities for brand extensions or new brands.

10
Glossary

Arbitrary Name
Names that do not bear a relationship to the products, services, or companies they identify. Apple (a fruit, not a computer), Pontiac (an Indian chief, not a car), Kodak (a coined name), and Baby Ruth (a person, not a candy bar) are all examples of arbitrary names.

Brand Architecture
The strategic analysis and development of optimal relationship structures among multiple levels of company, brand, product, and feature names.

Brand Name
A name or symbol used to identify a seller's goods or services, and to differentiate them from those of competitors. Because a brand identifies a product's or service's source, thus protecting against competitors who may attempt to market similar goods or services, companies have an incentive to invest in the quality, consistency, and imagery of their brand. Branding dates back to ancient times, when names or marks appeared on such goods as bricks, pots, ointments, and metals. In medieval Europe, trade guilds used brands to provide quality assurance for customers and legal protection for manufacturers.

Coined/Fanciful Name
These include made-up names such as Accenture or Kodak. Also known as neologisms. These names, if truly unique, can offer the strongest possible trademarks and are favored by trademark attorneys.

Consonant Cluster
A series of consonants pronounced together, e.g., /str/ in "string."

Customer Experience
It is the sum of all experiences a customer has with a supplier of goods or services over the duration of their relationship with that supplier, from awareness, discovery, attraction, interaction, purchase, use, and advocacy. It can also be used to mean an individual experience over one transaction; the distinction is usually clear in context.

Descriptive Name
A name that describes a product, service, or company. Descriptive names, such as Workgroup Server and Pacific Gas and Electric, have content, but often are not protectable and typically are not favored by trademark attorneys.

Descriptor
Often used in conjunction with a coined/fanciful, arbitrary, or suggestive name, a descriptor literally describes the product or service being identified. A brand name used with a variety of descriptors across a product line is often a more economic strategy than giving every product or service its own proprietary name.

Dilution

The legal doctrine of dilution, recognized in the statutes or case law of 31 states, applies to marks that are highly similar or identical to strong, well-known trademarks. The doctrine stipulates that the use of a famous trademark by any party other than its owner will result in loss of the mark's distinctiveness—even when the goods or services are not related and there is no likelihood of confusion. Some names may be judged to be available because they are already diluted; that is, the name is in use by a number of different companies, which may or may not include a famous user.

Full Legal Search

Trademark search conducted by trademark counsel, and encompassing all classes and countries of interest.

Intrinsic Meaning

The content or native sense or significance imparted by a word or name.

Linguistics

The study of the structure and development of a particular language and its relationship to other languages.

Morpheme

In linguistics, any word or word part that conveys meaning, that cannot be divided into smaller elements conveying meaning, and that usually occurs in a variety of contexts with relatively stable meaning.

Native Speakers Panel

Master-McNeil's group of recently arrived native speakers of a variety of languages. The panel reviews candidate names for international appropriateness including pronunciation issues, negative meanings, slang uses, and street or evolving language concerns in the languages of interest to the particular project.

Nomenclature System

A system that specifies and organizes the naming relationships among a company's brands, products, services, divisions, subsidiaries, and so on. A well-conceived nomenclature system will accommodate company growth and provide guidance for future product and service names. Some nomenclature systems are comprised of many levels, with specific naming guidelines for each.

Phoneme

In linguistics, a set of closely related speech sounds (phones) regarded as a single sound. For example, the sound of /r/ in *red*, *bring*, or *round* is a phoneme.

About the Author

Idris Mootee is the CEO of Idea Couture, a global strategic innovation firm with offices in North America, South America, Europe, and Asia. Idea Couture works with the world's leading brands to identify their highest-value brand-driven innovation opportunities, address their most critical challenges, develop breakthrough strategies, and create brand equities.

Mootee is a designer, marketer, writer, photographer, public speaker, publisher, business strategist, professor, management consultant, and board advisor. His mission is to bring the principles and processes of design thinking to all business disciplines, from branding and marketing to product development and experience design.

Prior to Idea Couture, Mootee held a number of top strategy positions, including SVP Global Head of Strategy for Blast Radius (WPP), Head of Strategy for Organic (OMNI), Head of Strategy N.A. for CBIZ Technologies (CBIZ), and EVP Head of Strategy for Live Lowe and Partners (IPG). He also designed and taught the Design Thinking for Business Innovation Executive Education Program at the Harvard Graduate School of Design and is a visiting professor for a number of business and design schools internationally. Mootee is a thought-provoking and highly sought-after global speaker on brand-led strategic innovation and new game strategy. He spends most of his time between London, San Francisco, Toronto, and Shanghai.

Index